SOLDIERS OF THE WHITE SUN

SOLDIERS OF THE WHITE SUN

THE CHINESE ARMY AT WAR
· 1931-1949 ·

Philip Jowett

Schiffer Military History
Atglen, PA

Acknowledgements

This book would not have been possible without the generous assistance of the following: Peter Hanff, David Harper, Peter Kengelbecher, Stefan Landsberger for permission to use posters from his collection, D.Y. Louie, Kevin Mahoney, Eric McChesney, James P. McNally, Alex De Quesada, Bin Shih for his kind permission to use photographs of small arms, and to Paul V. Walsh for his assistance over the years. The adapted color uniform plates and equipment sketches are used with the kind permission of the authors of *Chinese Infantry Uniforms & Equipment* (ISBN 957-30497-0-8). The color tank profiles are used with the kind permission of Janucz Ledwoch and were first featured in his book *Wojna Na Pacyfiku Daleki Wschod 1938-1945*.

Dedication

This book is respectfully dedicated to the ordinary soldiers of China who fought and suffered for their country during the long struggle against Japan from 1931 to 1945.

Book design by Robert Biondi.

Copyright © 2011 by Philip Jowett.
Library of Congress Catalog Number: 2011937316.

All rights reserved. No part of this work may be reproduced or used in any forms or by any means – graphic, electronic or mechanical, including photocopying or information storage and retrieval systems – without written permission from the publisher.

The scanning, uploading and distribution of this book or any part thereof via the Internet or via any other means without the permission of the publisher is illegal and punishable by law. Please purchase only authorized editions and do not participate in or encourage the electronic piracy of copyrighted materials.

"Schiffer," "Schiffer Publishing Ltd. & Design," and the "Design of pen and ink well" are registered trademarks of Schiffer Publishing, Ltd.

Printed in Hong Kong
ISBN: 978-0-7643-3956-1

We are always looking for people to write books on new and related subjects. If you have an idea for a book, please contact us at the address below.

Published by Schiffer Publishing Ltd.	In Europe, Schiffer books are distributed by:
4880 Lower Valley Road	Bushwood Books
Atglen, PA 19310	6 Marksbury Ave.
Phone: (610) 593-1777	Kew Gardens, Surrey TW9 4JF
FAX: (610) 593-2002	England
E-mail: Info@schifferbooks.com.	Phone: 44 (0)20 8392-8585
Visit our web site at: www.schifferbooks.com	FAX: 44 (0)20 8392-9876
Please write for a free catalog.	E-mail: info@bushwoodbooks.co.uk
This book may be purchased from the publisher.	www.bushwoodbooks.co.uk
Please include $5.00 postage.	
Try your bookstore first.	

Contents

Introduction........... 6
China at War: Chronology, 1928-1949........... 13

Manchuria, 1931-1932........... 20
Battle for Shanghai, January-March 1932........... 27
Japanese Invasion of Jehol, 1933........... 37
Civil Conflicts, 1933-1936........... 44
The Outbreak of the Sino-Japanese War, 1937........... 51
The Battle for Shanghai, August-October 1937........... 63
China's Agony Continues, October-December 1937........... 79
China's Continued Resistance, 1938-1941........... 87
The Chinese Army in Burma, 1942........... 104
China at War, 1942-1943........... 106
Allied Training Centres: Ramgarh and Yunnan, 1942-1943........... 120
Western China, 1943-1944........... 125
The Burmese Front, 1944-1945........... 130
The Chinese Homefront, 1944-1945........... 146
U.S. Training of Chinese Specialist Troops, 1944-1945........... 152
The Surrender of Imperial Japanese Forces in China, September 1945........... 154
Civil War, 1946-1949........... 156
Chinese Army Uniforms, Equipment and Weaponry, 1931-1949........... 173

INTRODUCTION

The Army of the Nationalist Government of China during the period covered by this book was almost constantly at war. From September 1931 when the Japanese invaded China's Manchurian provinces until the Nationalist defeat in the Civil War against the Chinese Communists in December 1949, they fought. Millions of Chinese soldiers served and died during this eighteen-year period, either fighting the Japanese or in internal conflicts between Nationalist factions or against the Communists. Many soldiers died in battle or from the wounds they received but others died in large numbers from neglect through hunger or disease. Chinese soldiers who usually came from peasant stock had the same stoical attitude to service in the army as he had to have working on the land for little reward. Although many fought patriotically for China especially against the Japanese others fought simply for the rice which was often the only payment they received. As was proven time and again the Chinese soldier when properly fed, equipped and trained was a match for the soldiers of any nation. Unfortunately the Chinese government was often incapable of, or unwilling to, provide what the soldier needed. This meant that the soldiers had to do the best they could with whatever resources they had and this often meant a shortage of arms, equipment, uniform and food. The millions of soldiers who fought and died for China between 1931 and 1949 are largely ignored in the military histories of the 20th Century. Likewise the contribution of the Chinese Army to the Allied war effort and the sacrifices they made between 1942 and 1945 are also have been largely overlooked. Because Japan would not give up its control of the Chinese homeland after 1942 they had to commit hundreds of thousands of troops to the theatre until their defeat in August 1945. Although badly led by most of their commanders and poorly supplied by their government the Chinese Army continued to fight. This book attempts to illustrate and describe the Chinese Nationalist Army during this traumatic and decisive period in the world's and the nation's history.

The Chinese Nationalist Army, 1931-1945

The Chinese Army that faced the Japanese Invasion of Manchuria in 1931 was a reduced and reorganised version of the National Revolutionary Army which had only recently defeated the Northern Warlords in the Northern Expedition of 1926-1928. In 1929 there were 1,620,000 men under arms with many having little or no loyalty to Chiang Kai-shek. Many troops were under the command of former warlords who had thrown in their lot with the NRA during the Northern Expedition. The size of the Army could not be sustained by the Chinese Government especially when the loyalty of many units was suspect. A disbandment policy was quickly instituted to reduce this force to a sixty-five division army with each division having 11,000 men. Rebellions throughout 1929-1930 by former allies of the Nationalists caused partly by the disbandment policy were eventually put down by Chiang Kai-shek and his loyal troops.

Importantly for Chiang the Manchurian Warlord Chang Hsueh-liang expressed his loyalty and that of his troops to the Nationalist government in 1930. Chang Hsueh-liang 'The Young Marshal' was the son of Chang Tso-lin main opponent of the Northern Expedition who had been assassinated by his Japanese sponsors in 1928. When the Japanese invaded Manchuria in November 1931 the 160,000 Chinese troops stationed there were under the command of Chang Hsueh-liang. Chang had received orders from Chiang Kai-shek not to resist the invasion so that the Japanese would be judged to be the aggressors. Widespread resistance to the Japanese by 250,000 guerrillas who were former soldiers as well as patriotic volunteers did break out. This resistance, which received no government support, caused the Japanese problems until they finally defeated the anti-Japanese volunteers armies in 1933. Chiang Kai-shek however was distracted from the loss of Manchuria by his obsession with defeating his Communist enemies. The Communists had set up several armed 'Soviets' or bases from where they intended to resist the Nationalists. From 1930 until 1934 a series of five Extermination Campaigns were launched by the Nationalists employing hundreds of thousands of the best troops of the Nationalist Army. These troops many argued would have been better employed in the north of China fighting the Japanese. Because of the concentration of the better Nationalist units against the Communists when the Japanese next invaded Jehol province in 1933 they were again faced with regional troops poorly armed and equipped.

Chiang realised that his army needed to be modernised and reorganised if it was to be capable of defeating the Communists as well as resisting any further Japanese attacks. According to the 1934 League of Nations report, the strength of the Chinese Army in December 1933 was 1,316,580 men. The Army was made up of 134 Infantry Divisions, thirty-three Independent Infantry Brigades, six Independent Infantry Regiments, eight Cavalry Divisions, and fourteen Independent Cavalry Brigades. Other units included four brigades, nineteen regiments and nine companies of artillery and 9,000 Military Police in five regiments. This large army was basically an infantry force with little artillery and few up-to-date weapons. As part of his modernisation plans Chiang decided to employ a number of German military advisors.

German advisors had been in China in small numbers since the late-1920s but with the arrival of former Marshal Hans von Seekt the military mission expanded. Von Seekt had been responsible for the superb organisation of the 100,000 strong restricted Army of the German Weimer Republic after 1918. Under his leadership the China Mission grew to sixty-one staff in 1933 and at its height in 1935 to seventy advisors. When von Seekt left China in 1936 due to ill health he was replaced by the capable General Alexander von Falkenhausen. The plan was for the mission to eventually train twenty infantry divisions by 1937-1938 and to go on to organise and train all of the army, navy and air force by the early-1940s. Germany's new found friendship with the Japanese from 1936 was to alter this however with only thirty military advisors in China in 1938 who had all left the country by July that year. Before they were withdrawn the mission had managed to fully train eight infantry divisions including the 'elite' 83rd, 87th and 88th Divisions. In further attempts to modernise the Army, China imported modern artillery pieces and anti-aircraft guns from Germany and Sweden. These included forty-eight 105mm and forty-four 150mm German field guns, as well as seventy-two Swedish Bofors 75mm mountain guns. Tanks were purchased in Germany, Britain and Italy. Additional weaponry came from various European arms manufacturers as well.

Up to date German scout cars were also bought to equip a few 'showpiece' units. Small arms in particular came from every available source as the Chinese had to supplement what their own arms factories could produce. At the same time an 80,000 strong military training force was established which was planned to be the nucleus of the new modern army.

When the Sino-Japanese War broke out in July 1937 the Chinese Nationalist Army had an 'on paper' strength of 1,700,000 men. This force was made up of 182 Infantry Divisions, forty-six Independent Infantry Brigades and nine Cavalry Divisions. Other units were made up of six Independent Cavalry Brigades, and Artillery units were made up of four brigades and twenty regiments. Mechanised units were made up of a few companies with only a few dozen tanks and armoured cars. The Nationalist Army divisions varied in strength and quality with units varying in size from the official 10,000 men down to only 5,000 men. Loyalty to the government was a strong decider in how much training, equipment and weaponry a division would get with about 380,000 men in the best and loyalist units. Another 520,000 men were in less well-equipped and trained divisions which had some loyalty to the Central Government of Chiang Kai-shek. Other divisions and brigades which made up an additional 300,000 men were stationed in the outlying provinces of China and had little or no loyalty to Chiang's government. These 'semi-autonomous provincial troops' could only be relied on to fight in defence of their own region and then only if it suited their commander to order their participation. The modernisation plans for the army had made some improvements and they did have some modern weaponry but not in sufficient amounts.

During the first two years of the Sino-Japanese War the Chinese Army suffered catastrophic losses in both men and equipment. Most of the best-trained and equipped divisions were lost during the 1937-1938 fighting when Chiang Kai-shek tried to take on the Japanese in conventional warfare. Attempts were made in 1938 and 1939 to replace these heavy losses with recruitment drives and although new soldiers could be trained the quality of the army could not be maintained. Not only had precious heavy weaponry been lost but the high casualty rates amongst junior officers further weakened the army. After the withdrawal of German arms shipments after 1937 a new source of weaponry had to be found. The signing of a non-aggression pact with the Soviet Union in July 1937 bore fruit for the Chinese however. From September 1937 until June 1941 the Soviet Union supplied China with $173,000,000 worth of tanks, artillery and aircraft. Russia's intention was to keep the Chinese in the war so they could tie down Japanese troops that could be used to attack them in Siberia, as they had in 1919-1922. Even with substantial Soviet arms supplies Chiang knew that the only strategy available to him in 1938-1941 was to conduct a fighting withdrawal. A fighting retreat would allow the government to remove as many people and industry to the safety of western China. This 'scorched earth' policy was to use China's vast territory to extend the Japanese Imperial Army's supply lines and wear them down. Although the period from 1938 until 1941 saw heavy losses by the Chinese they were not on the scale of the early fighting. By 1941 the Chinese Army even after its losses of the previous four years fighting stood at 2,919,000 front line troops in 246 divisions and forty-four independent brigades. There were also an additional 900,000 troops in seventy divisions and three brigades which were stationed in the outlying and rear areas. These troops could be regarded as 'second-line' and mostly had little combat value as they were poorly trained and equipped.

Divisions had a 1941 official establishment of 9,529 men with 324 machine guns but most were under strength in both men and weaponry. By 1942 the Japanese were trying to find some kind of peace agreement with Chiang Kai-shek in order to release troops for the Pacific Theatre. Even though the Chinese Army was at a low ebb at this time with most units suffering severe shortages of weaponry and equipment, Chiang was adamant that the war should continue.

Chiang had managed to keep some of his surviving better units in reserve for the expected renewal of the war against the Communists. These better units included the 5th and 6th Armies some of which had been trained and partly equipped by the Germans in the 1930s. Other reliable units in Chiang's Army included sixteen armies from North-Western China which had been largely untouched by the fighting. After the outbreak of the fighting between the Japanese and British Army in Burma in early 1942, nine Divisions from the 5th and 6th Armies were sent across the border from China. Chiang had reluctantly agreed to send some of his best divisions to the British in an attempt to protect his supply lines through Burma. After the defeat of the British in May 1942 the remaining Chinese Units withdrew back to China or into India. Those units that withdrew to India included the 'elite' 20th and 38th Divisions and these were to form the core of a new army trained and equipped by the U.S. and British. The units trained in India and in the U.S. training camps in Western China between 1942-1945 were well trained and equipped. They formed a new 'elite' force within the Chinese Army in the same way that the German trained divisions did in the 1930s. Unfortunately they were only a small fraction of the Chinese Army the majority of who were still badly trained, armed and equipped. General Stilwell in a summary of the state of the Chinese Army in September 1943 told Chiang Kai-shek that many of their 300 divisions had not seen any combat. He estimated that only ten percent of the divisions were commanded by officers who had strong loyalty to Chiang. In his opinion the rest of the divisions were under the command of generals who had loyalty to their own regional leaders or governors. When it came to material he said that there were about 1,000,000 rifles, 83,000 machine guns and 7,800 trench mortars in service. Most of the 1,330 Artillery pieces in China were not held centrally and those in the hands of regional commanders were jealously guarded and not risked in battles. By 1944 the oversize army had an official strength of 5,700,000 men many who served in rear units and this number had to be reduced. On paper there were 324 divisions, sixty or so brigades and eighty-nine so-called guerrilla units with an average strength of 2,000 men each.

The Nationalist Army in the Civil War, 1946-1949

During late 1944 up to April 1945 there was a reduction of 1,410 units of various sizes and designation which took 1,100,000 men off the payroll. Many of the surplus soldiers were then re-assigned to combat units which increased front line strength by 150,000. The end of the Second World War in August 1945 left the Chinese government with a 3,000,000 strong army which was again too large for the exhausted nation to finance. Even though a renewed civil war with the Communists was certain the Nationalist government had to rationalise its army into a slightly more manageable 2,400,000 men.

Out of this force about 1,700,000 were combat troops and as was usual in Chinese military history these troops varied greatly in effectiveness. Some of the Nationalist Divisions had been trained and equipped by the USA during World War II while others were no better than lightly armed militia. U.S. promises to equip a thirty-nine division strong force which was to form the core of the 'new' Chinese Army had been completed by the winter of 1945-1946. In 1946 the Nationalists had the same pre-1945 mixture of good and bad units with the best divisions including the U.S. trained 'New 1st' and 'New 6th' Divisions. Other good divisions were the so-called Youth Divisions which had been formed in the last years of the Second World War from student volunteers.

Although the Nationalists had a relatively well-equipped army which most observers believed would be strong enough to defeat the Communists there were many weaknesses. The regular army depended on support from locally recruited and lightly armed paramilitaries known as the Peace Preservation Corps. Other second-line troops were made up of various armed police forces including units responsible for the defence of the railway system. Some second line troops had been relatively well supplied with modern weaponry with 423,422 small arms and 17,253 machine guns being supplied from July 1946 to January 1949. Many of these arms ended up in Communist hands as second line troops were even less reliable than the regular army and could easily be persuaded to change sides. Morale in the Nationalist Army was often affected by the poor treatment that the ordinary soldier still received. Medical care was still grossly inadequate with no lessons leant from the way that Chinese soldiers had been treated pre-1945. Corruption was rife amongst the poorly paid officers who sold rice meant for their troops to supplement their income. Some officers even charged their men for rice which they should have received as part of their rations! Although there were as always good officers they were in the minority and many officers were poorly trained political appointees. As with the 1931-1945 period it was noted that when well treated the average Nationalist soldier was willing to fight. Nationalist troops who defected to the enemy did not do so generally because they were pro-Communist but because they were promised, and received better treatment.

U.S. heavy weaponry was supplied to the Nationalists during the Civil War including modern 75mm, 105mm howitzers and 155mm howitzers. Armoured vehicles were not however supplied in large numbers by the U.S. with the majority being M3A3 light tanks. Tanks like the M4 Sherman were considered too heavy to travel along the poor roads and cross the ramshackle bridges of China. The rest of the Nationalists heavy equipment was made up of Japanese tanks and artillery taken as war booty in 1945. At the beginning of the Civil War the Nationalists enjoyed a massive advantage on paper over the Communists in both numbers of men and in weaponry. They had a 3 to 1 advantage in numbers of soldiers in 1946 as well as a total superiority in artillery. By the middle of 1947 the Communist army had 1,950,000 troops and the Nationalists had 3,730,000. But many were assigned to garrison duty in re-conquered areas. Because the Communists had no aircraft of their own at the start of the Civil War the Nationalists also had complete air superiority. These very real advantages were soon to prove insufficient to defeat the better-motivated Communists. The artillery and armour the Nationalists had were poorly employed by them and often fell into enemy hands. As the Civil War progressed the Nationalists lost their advantages over the Communists as they were defeated in battle losing both men and weaponry to the enemy. Nationalist defeats in Manchuria in 1948 saw them lose the best U.S. trained divisions and their U.S. supplied equipment. After the decisive battles of 1948 the pendulum swung in the Communists favour as men and weapons were captured in huge numbers.

From the period from July 1946 until January 1949 the Communists claimed to have taken 3,700,000 prisoners. The liberal policy adopted by the Communists which allowed Nationalist troops to join their army without any repercussions led to large scale defections. During the same period the Nationalists lost 580 tanks, 360 armoured cars, 60,000 artillery pieces of all types as well as 250,000 machine guns and two-million small arms. By early 1949 the Nationalists were suffering real shortages of small arms for the first time which affected recruitment. Even when last ditch efforts were made to recruit a mass militia in the Peking region there were not sufficient arms to equip them with. Ammunition was also in short supply. As early as December 1947 only twenty-two days supply of 7.92mm, and thirty-six days supply of U.S. .30 for the M1 carbine ammunition were available for the army. Unfortunately for the desperate Nationalists they were often forced to pay over the odds for arms with U.S. army surplus M2 carbines selling for $5.00 in the States being charged to the Chinese at $51.00 each! As 1949 progressed the news for the Nationalists got worse by the day and by June they only had 1,500,000 troops, regular and irregular left. This shortage of troops was not helped by Chiang Kai-shek's decision to withdraw some of his best units to the island of Taiwan where he was preparing his 'bastion'. In reality by mid-1949 Chiang had given up on defeating the Communists and had decided to retreat to Taiwan as a 'temporary' measure. The Nationalist troops that went to Taiwan with Chiang proved sufficient to stop a Communist takeover of the island. At the same time the Nationalist Army would never be strong enough to return to the mainland and 'liberate' the people of China.

Unit Organisation, 1931-1949

During the period 1931-1949 the Chinese Nationalist Army's unit strengths were changed on several occasions. After the re-organisation of the Nationalist Army in 1928-1929 there were three types of divisions introduced – these were the A, B and C. The 1929 'A' Type Division had an official strength of 11,720 men and 805 officers with two infantry brigades with each having three regiments. Type 'B' Divisions had 11,749 men with 818 officers in three infantry brigades with each having two regiments in them. The Type 'C' Division was smaller with 8,357 men and 586 officers in two infantry brigades with each made up of two infantry regiments. Support units in the 'A' and 'B' Divisions consisted of one artillery battalion, one engineer battalion, one transport battalion and a cavalry squadron. Type 'C' Divisions had more artillery with a regiment made up of three battalions with an official strength of twelve field guns in three batteries. Some adjustments were made to the divisional structure during the early- to mid-1930s with a new type of division formed as part of the Anti-Communist Encirclement campaigns of 1930-1934. The new type divisional structure was based on the 1929 Type 'C' with some small adjustments and was only used on units involved in the Anti-Communist campaigns. All other divisions were officially to be based on the Type 'A' or 'B' structure but as with all Chinese military organisation in the 1930s this may have only been 'on paper'. By 1937 when the Sino-Japanese War began some divisions were re-organised and had a strength of 10,265 men and 658 officers. The official weaponry of the 1937 Division was supposed to be 3,821 rifles, 243 hand grenade launchers, 247 light machine guns and fifty-four heavy machine guns. Heavy weaponry used by the division was supposed to be sixteen field guns/howitzers and thirty medium mortars.

In 1942 as part of a rationalisation of the Nationalist Army which saw a forty percent reduction in the number of units a new divisional organisation was introduced which had a strength of 6,428 soldiers and 366 officers. This figure was closer to the actual strength that most pre-1942 divisions had attained during 1937-1942. At the end of the war a new proposed 1945 division was suggested with a strength of 10,309 men and 668 officers. The situation from 1945 until the start of the Civil War did not allow for much reorganisation and all the tinkering with unit strengths did not achieve a lot. During the Civil War the average division had an establishment of roughly 10,000 men who were nearly all infantry. Most divisions had only a single battalion of artillery armed with a mixture of Japanese and U.S. field guns. Smaller units within the division varied in size from unit to unit with Peace Preservation Corps militia often making up any losses during the war. China's military organisation at the highest level during the 1937-1945 period was based on a series of War 'Zones' or War Regions. These War Zones were geographically based and usually covered several adjoining provinces. War Zone commanders who were like the pre-1928 Warlord had overall command of all the military units within their provinces. They were supposed to have overall responsibility for any military operations in their region but this caused problems at times. War Zones were fluid and changed at various times during the Sino-Japanese War as the territory controlled by the Nationalist government shrank. The largest field formation of the Chinese Army during the Sino-Japanese War was the Army Group. Army Groups were made up of two or more Armies which were made up of two or more corps. Army corps consisted of two or more divisions which of course varied greatly in size from 5,000 to nearly 12,000 men.

During the Civil War the Nationalist formations were organised into regional War Zones known as commands and were given the title of their nearest city, e.g. 'Peking Command'. These regional commands consisted of several Corps which had two or three field divisions with official strengths of 10,977 men each. The reality was that a typical Nationalist Division had about half the official strength. From 1946 divisions were given the new designation 'Reorganised Brigade' with two regiments per unit. After May 1947 there was supposed be an additional regiment added to each brigade but this may not have happened. To confuse matters, in September 1948 the Reorganised Brigades again became divisions. In reality all these changes came to little and a typical division and brigade had a strength of approximately 5,000 men.

CHINA AT WAR: CHRONOLOGY 1928-1949

1928-1930
The end of the Northern Expedition in 1928 sees Chiang Kai-shek and his Kuomintang Nationalist Party in control of the whole of China. Starting in 1926 the Northern Expedition by the Kuomintang's National Revolutionary Army was a campaign to unite the whole of China by defeating the regional warlords who had controlled the country since 1916. Some warlords are defeated while others choose to bring their armies over to the Nationalist cause and claim loyalty to Chiang Kai-shek. In reality the new government is far from secure with the main danger coming from rebellions led by Chiang's former allies. Firstly in 1929 war breaks out between Feng Yu-hsiang the 'Christian Warlord' who had joined Chiang during the Northern Expedition. Then after Feng's defeat he joins with the 'Shansi Warlord' Yen His-shan as well as Nationalist politicians in opposition to Chiang Kai-shek. They call a conference in Peking in September 1930 which proclaims a new Nationalist government and calls for Chiang Kai-shek's overthrow. However Chiang with the military support of the 'Young Marshal' Chang Hsueh-liang defeats the rebellion and sends Feng and Yen into temporary exile. The military campaign to defeat the rebellion in 1930, known as the Central Plains War is very costly with 300,000 casualties in total.

1930
October - 1st Nationalist Encirclement Campaign against the Communists in the so-called 'Kiangsu Soviet' is unsuccessful. The Communists have set up several base areas since the late-1920s and Chiang Kai-shek is determined to destroy them. Nationalist forces involved were about 100,000 men but they were defeated by about 40,000 Communists. The Nationalist commander was captured and beheaded by the victorious Communists.

1931
April-May - 2nd Encirclement Campaign involving 200,000 Nationalist troops against the Communist's 30,000 men. Again the Communists were victorious capturing 20,000 rifles which enabled them to expand their forces. **August-September** - 3rd Encirclement Campaign is launched with estimates of up to 300,000 Nationalists trying to defeat between 30,000-55,000 Communists. This third attempt by the Nationalists to eliminate the Communists ended largely in a stalemate with both sides suffering heavy losses. The Japanese invasion of Manchuria distracted both sides from the fighting as more pressing matters unfolded. **September 18th** - Mukden Incident, the destruction of a section of the Japanese controlled South Manchuria Railway by their own agents is used as a pretext for the takeover of Manchuria. The Japanese Kwangtung Army made up of only just over a division's worth of troops on its own initiative advances across Manchuria meeting minimal resistance from its Chinese garrisons. Chinese troops under the overall command of the 'Young Marshal' Chang Hsueh-liang are told not to resist and are mostly disarmed by the Japanese.

1932
January - Japanese proclaim the new state of Manchukuo with the last Emperor of China Pu-Yi as 'chief executive'. **January-May** - Shanghai incident in which the Japanese invade large parts of the city and battle the Chinese 19th Route Army. Chiang Kai-shek then transfers the 19th to remoter Fukien Province to avoid its commander, General Tsai Ting-kai becoming a possible political rival. **February** - The Kwangtung Army's conquest of the whole of Manchuria is completed.

1933
January 1st - An incident staged by the Kwangtung Army leads to the Japanese demanding the withdrawal of the Nationalist 626th Regiment from its defensive positions at Shanhaiguan which protect the Great Wall. **January-March** - Japanese invasion of Jehol Province bordering Manchuria leads to the provinces absorption into Manchukuo. The Chinese forces defending Jehol consist of the 4th, 5th and 6th Army Groups totalling about 50,000 men. When the Japanese attack several Chinese cavalry commanders defect with their men to the other side. **April** - 4th Encirclement Campaign involving an initial Nationalist force of seventeen divisions totalling 154,000 men against 65,000 Communists. The Communists

knowing that the Nationalists would soon be reinforced in strength, attack and defeat Chiang Kai-shek's forces. Having failed in four attempts to defeat the Communists the Nationalists change tactics under the guidance of German military advisors for their next and final campaign against them. **November** - Start of Fukien Rebellion involving 19th Route Army which had been moved to the province from Shanghai after its valiant resistance to the Japanese in 1932.

1934
January - End of Fukien Rebellion, leaders go into exile. **April-October** - 5th Encirclement Campaign successfully blockades the Communists who know they will have to break out of their base in Kwangsi to survive. **October 20th** - Long March begins with 100,000 men, women and children escaping the Nationalist blockade with the intention of reaching a new base in far off Yenan in Shensi Province.

1935
October - Communists reach new secure base in Yenan but have suffered about 90,000 losses by death and desertion during the march. Casualties are caused by continual Nationalist and bandit attacks throughout the Communist retreat as well as by hunger and disease.

1936
June-July - Anti-Chiang Kai-shek revolt by Generals Ch'en Chi-t'ang and Li Chi-shen in Kwangtung and the three Kwangsi Generals, Li Tsung-jen, Pai Ch'ung-his and Huang Shao-hsiung is defeated by the Nationalist government. **October** - Prince Te Wang the leader of the independence movement in the Chinese region of Inner Mongolia accepts Japanese support including military advisors, tanks, artillery and planes. He leads a 15,000 strong army of mixed Manchurian and Mongolians into Suiyuan province in an attempt to wrest it from Nationalist control. The prince is hoping to create an 'independent' Inner Mongolian state out of several North-Western Chinese provinces. **November 24th** - Local Chinese forces under the command of General Fu Tso-yi take the Inner Mongolian headquarters at Pailingmiao capturing equipment and documents which prove Japanese complicity with the rebels. This defeat of Japanese sponsored forces is hailed in China as a victory, albeit by 'proxy' over the Imperial Army. **December 12th** - 'Sian Incident' - Chiang Kai-shek is kidnapped by several of his generals when on a visit to his troops in Sian. He flew there to insist that their troops begin an anti-Communist campaign which they had been stalling on. After the defeat of the proxy Mongolian troops in October a mood of anti-Japanese resistance had swept through China. The rebel generals insisted that Chiang agree to form a United Front with the Communists to fight the Japanese.

1937
July 7th - Marco Polo Bridge Incident - clashes between Chinese and Japanese troops in the region of this historic bridge is used as a pretext by the Japanese to launch a full-scale invasion of China. **July 17th** - Chiang Kai-shek expresses his desire for peace with Japan but also states that if this is not possible China will fight to the bitter end. **July 31st** - Peking falls to Japanese. **August 13th to late-October** - *Battle of Shanghai* - Chinese forces defending the city total about 600,000 men and are attacked by 300,000 Japanese. Heavy casualties are suffered by both sides with the Chinese losing up to half of their men killed or wounded. **September-October** - Japanese and 'puppet' Inner Mongolian forces advance into the provinces of Chahar and Suiyuan. **October 10th** - Fall of Shihchiachuang to Japanese. **October 13th to November 2nd** - *Battle of Sinkow* - Japanese attempts to take Taiyuan the capital of Shansi province were resisted by strong Chinese forces. The Japanese after a hard battle retire southwards **November 8th** - Chinese High Command finally orders withdrawal of all forces in the Shanghai area. Surviving Nationalist troops retreat towards Nanking with some troops joining the defences of the capital. **November 8th- 9th** - Fall of Taiyuan in Shansi Province. **November 19th** - Fall of Soochow west of Shanghai. **December 13th** - Fall of Nationalist capital Nanking which had been defended by an ad-hoc force of about 100,000 men made up of newly raised troops and some units

who had withdrawn from the Shanghai battle. The fall of the city was followed by the execution of all the thousands of Chinese prisoners of war taken during the battle. The Japanese Imperial Army then begin wholesale massacres of the civilian population with over 300,000 people killed, tortured and raped. Atrocities that take place in Nanking in the weeks following the fall of the city are some of the worse outrages seen during the 20th Century. **December** - Nationalists move their capital to Wuhan in Hupeh Province.

1938

March-April - *Battle of Taierhchung* - In a rare victory, units of the Chinese 2nd Group Army under the command of General Li Tsung-jen defeat the Japanese 10th Division at Taierhchuang in Shantung Province. Both sides suffer equally heavy losses during the bitter street fighting for the town with a rough figure of 16,000 men per army. The Japanese escaped from the battle with only 2,000 men in their most humiliating defeat of the war. **April** - Nationalist programme calls for political training in the Chinese Army to be intensified and for all able-bodied citizens in Free China to be given some form of military training. **April 28th** - Germany cancels all arms shipments including existing contracts to China. **May** - The coastal city of Swatow defended only by second-line units and the island of Amoy fall to Japanese amphibious landings in quick succession. **June 6th** - Japanese take Kaifeng in Honan Province and would have gone on to take the rest of the province but Chiang Kai-shek orders the blowing up of the Yellow River dikes. This floods large parts of the province and kills thousands of civilians but stops the Japanese advance. **June 13th to October 25th** - Defence of Hankow, the epic defence of the 'new' capital of China after the fall of Nanking lasted almost five months. The 800,000 Chinese troops defending the city are affected by an outbreak of a malaria epidemic. The fall of the nearby city of Kukiang on the 26th of July and the atrocities committed there by the Japanese further affect morale. After the government withdraws from the city in early September resistance continues until late October when it falls to the Japanese. **October 12th-21st** - Japanese take the city of Canton in the south of China, the last major seaport available to the Chinese government which was defended by the 12th Army Group. The city fell to the 70,000 strong Japanese force which had been landed by the Imperial Navy with little resistance by the defending force. **October 25th** - Japanese take the tri-city area of Wuhan where Chiang Kai-shek's HQ is situated and the Chinese lose 100 aircraft and 200,000 casualties during the battle. The Nationalists move their capital westwards to distant Chungking in Szechwan Province which becomes the wartime capital until 1945.

1939

February 10th - Hainan Island off the Chinese southern coast falls to a Japanese amphibious force. **March** - The strategically vital Burma Road is opened for military traffic. **March 17th to late April** - *Battle of Nanchang* - in Kiangsi Province, The city defended by 200,000 Chinese regular and irregular troops was surrounded by the 27th of March by 120,000 Japanese. Chinese attacks to relieve the city during April were eventually defeated with their losses reaching over 50,000. **April 20th to May 24th** - *Battle of Sui Hsien-Tsaoyang*, - after the Japanese victory at Wuhan they moved four divisions southwards towards the two cities in Northern Hupeh province from which the battle is named and clashed with large Chinese forces. Although the Chinese withdrew in front of the Japanese advance General Li Tsung-jen took two army corps behind them and forced them to withdraw in turn. The battle ended in a rare Chinese victory with casualties on their side of 9,000 while the Japanese reportedly lost 13,000 men. **May** - Japanese bombing raids begin against Chungking with the first two days raids killing 4,400 people. Over the next three years the Japanese air force bombed the Chinese wartime capital 268 times. **September 14th** - *1st Battle of Changsha*, - This first battle to fall into the timeframe of the Second World War ends with the Japanese unable to take the city. Although the Chinese defence force at 180,000 was twice the size of the Japanese attacking force this was still a vital victory for the Nationalists. **November 1939 to March 1940** - The Chinese launch multiple offensives across nine provinces in north, central and south China in what is commonly called the 1939-1940 *'Winter Offensive'*. Over half a million largely untried Chinese troops were launched against superior Japanese forces. The offensive's main aim of throwing the

Japanese off balance and stopping any further advances by them is a failure. Estimates of Chinese casualties vary between 70,000-80,000 with Japanese casualties about 20,000 dead and wounded. **November** - Japanese invade Kwangsi province. **December 18th to January 11th 1940** - *Battle of Kunlun Pass* - A Japanese offensive in Kwangsi province to try and cut off China from supplies from French Indo-China was countered by a 60,000 strong Chinese force. The Chinese 5th Corps had a number of recently supplied Soviet tanks and armoured cars with which to attack the 45,000 Japanese force. Although the victorious Chinese suffered 14,000 casualties the Japanese lost 8,000 men including a high proportion of officers.

1940

September - Under heavy Japanese pressure the beleaguered British government closes the Burma Road as the Imperial government tries to stop any supplies reaching the Chinese. **October** - Japanese finally withdraw from Kwangsi after being unable to consolidate their position there and the Chinese retake the city of Nanning. **October** - Britain re-opens Burma Road.

1941

January 4th-7th - The '*New Fourth Army Incident*' takes place as 40,000 Nationalist troops attack Communist units under their command. The Communists suffer 4,000 soldiers killed in running battles with the Nationalists as well as 5,000 civilian deaths and the attack ends the always un-easy anti-Japanese alliance between the Nationalists and the Communists. From now on both conduct their own campaigns and begin fighting against each other as well as against the Japanese. **January 17th** - Chiang Kai-shek orders the disbandment of the New Fourth Army and the arrest of its commander. **March 15th-28th** - *Battle of Shangkao* - A 65,000 strong Japanese force with forty armoured cars and strong air cover attacked the HQ of the 100,000 strong Chinese 11th Army in Kiangsi province. Both sides suffered heavy losses of about 20,000 men each and the Japanese withdrew from the region leaving behind substantial supplies. **May 7th-21st** - *Battle of Southern Shansi* - 100,000 strong Japanese force attempts to dislodge 180,000 Chinese troops of the 5th and 14th Army Groups along with five other Corps. The Chinese are holding positions in the Chungtiaoshan Range from which they are eventually forced to retire after heavy fighting on the 12th of May. **September 8th** - *2nd Battle of Changsha* - again the Japanese fail to take the city. **October 11th** - Chinese briefly retake Ichang in Hupeh Province. **November 1st** - Chinese retake Chengchow in Honan Province. **December 7th** - Japanese attack on Pearl Harbour brings the USA into the war against Japan and leads to the four year long Sino-Japanese War being absorbed into the greater conflict. Over the next five months Japanese Imperial forces launch a highly successful lightning campaign to conquer British Hong Kong, Malaya and Burma as well as the U.S. defended Philippines and the Dutch East Indies. The Japanese offensive into Burma threatens to isolate China from its only remaining supply lines along the Burma Road.

1942

January - Two divisional strength Chinese Armies, the 5th and 6th advance into Northern Burma to support the beleaguered British forces fighting the Japanese there. **March 21st-30th** - The Chinese 200th Division equipped with Soviet supplied T-26 tanks holds the Japanese 55th Division at Toungoo in Northern Burma. **April 11th-19th** - In Burma just over 1,100 men of the 113th Regiment of the Chinese 38th Division marched to break the encirclement of the British 1st Burma Division at Yenangyaung. 7,000 British troops were surrounded by approximately 7,000 Japanese of the 33rd Division. Chinese troops were supported by British Stuart tanks and artillery that had been assigned to the rescue force. The relieved British had to leave their heavy weapons behind and along with their Chinese allies were forced by heavy Japanese pressure to withdraw northward. **April** - General Stilwell suggests that 100,000 Chinese troops be sent to Ramgarh in India for training and equipping with U.S. Lend Lease armaments. Chiang Kai-shek agrees and the 22nd and 38th Divisions who have just fought in Burma plus some smaller units eventually arrive at the training camps. **May 11th** - Tengchung in Western Yunnan falls to Japanese. **August 28th**

- Chinese troops recapture Chuhsien and recover most of the length of the Chekiang-Kiangsi Railway. **1942** - During the year fifteen Nationalist generals decided to go over to the Japanese side and took approximately 500,000 men with them. The number of generals defecting to the Japanese rose to forty-two the following year along with hundreds of thousands of men. Some suggested that Chiang Kai-shek was using the Japanese temporarily to feed his troops who were mostly used in fighting the Communists.

1943

February - Chiang Kak-shek agrees to the employment of Chinese troops in the re-conquest of Burma and in return asks for a big increase in U.S. military aid. **May-June** - Hupeh Operation by Chinese involves the defence of Chungking from a perceived threat by the Japanese. When the Japanese decide to withdraw their forces the pro-Chinese press claims a major victory for the Chungking regime. **August** - U.S. trained troops from the Ramgarh training facilities known as 'X' Force invade northern Burma. **November** - Kweilin Infantry Training Center opened, with 2,200 U.S. personnel to train Chinese troops for the proposed thirty division strong 'Z' - Zebra Force. 'Z' Force was intended to defend airbases in eastern China and to eventually undertake a counter-offensive against Japanese forces in the Yangtze valley. **December 3rd-9th** - Japanese troops capture Changteh in North-Western Hunan on the 3rd but it is retaken by the Chinese six days later.

1944

May 11th - The U.S. trained Chinese Expeditionary Force (C.E.F.) (also known as 'Y' Force) in Western Yunnan succeed in establishing bridgehead on the west bank of the River Salween. **May 11th-12th** - Operations by C.E.F. ('Y' Force) fail to re-open Burma Road. **May 26th** - Main phase of Japanese 'Ichi-go' offensive begins with drive southwards by Japanese 11th Army while the 23rd Army attacked westward from Canton. The main objective of the offensive was to destroy U.S. airbases in China that could strike against Japan. **May-August** - Siege of Myitkhina by Allied forces including Chinese 30th and 38th Divisions of the New 1st Army - part of 'X' Force. **June 18th** - Changsha falls to Japanese after the three previous attempts to take the town had failed. **June 26th** - Hengyang the site of an important U.S. airbase is attacked by the advancing Japanese but is held by the garrison made up 15,000 men of the Chinese 10th Army. **August 8th** - After a six-week battle Hengyang finally falls to the Japanese. **September 6th** - Special Units of the Chinese Expeditionary Force ('Y' Force) in Western Yunnan and the Chinese Army in India ('X' Force) which are fighting in northern Burma meet up. They meet on the Kaoliangkung Pass which is the border between China and Burma. **September 14th** - Chinese forces launch a final attack on the walled city of Tengchung in western Yunnan which has been under siege for fifty-one days and take it next day. The Japanese were reported to have lost 3,000 during the battle. **November 6th** - 22nd Division crosses Irrawaddy River and overcomes weak Japanese resistance at Shwegugale. **November 10th** - Kweilin falls to Japanese. **November 30th** - Chaing Kai-shek asks for 22nd Division of 'Y' Force to be withdrawn from Burma to reinforce the 14th Division defending Kunming. **December 1st** - Chinese take Chefang on Salween Front. **December 15th** - Fall of Bhamo on northern Burma Front which is taken by Chinese New 1st Army which had advanced further south after taking Myitkhina.

1945

January 3rd - 9th Division of 2nd Nationalist Army enters Wanting on the border between Burma and China and are then driven out again. **January 17th** - 38th Division begins mopping up Japanese on the road beyond Myitkyina. **February 4th** - First convoy along the Stilwell Road arrives in Kunming. **March** - Chinese advance in Burma is halted on the orders of Chiang Kai-shek who says they cannot go beyond the Lashio-Hsipaw-Kyaukse line. **April 8th - Early May** - *Chihchiang Offensive* – Japan's last offensive in China is launched by the 20th Army from territory recently captured during ICHIGO. The target of the offensive was the major U.S. airbase at Chihchiang and four divisional sized Chinese armies defended it. After being reinforced by two more divisions the Japanese were finally halted and pushed back to their starting point. **May** - Japanese forces in China begin to withdraw from outlying garrisons and are told to concentrate their forces in North China, the Lower Yangtze region and the Canton - Hong Kong area. **June 22nd** - Chinese take the town of Liuchow but not before the retreating Japanese have burned it to the ground. **June 26th** - Chinese capture Liuchow Airfield. **July 27th** - Chinese troops enter Kweilin but Japanese continue fighting for a few days. **August 5th** - Chinese 13th Army captures Tanchuk and the 58th Division liberates Hsinning. **September 2nd** - Japanese formally surrender and in the major cities in central and southern China Nationalist forces take over from the defeated enemy. **September 9th** - Japanese General Yasuji Okamura C-in-C of the Chinese Expeditionary Forces signs a surrender document on behalf of over one-million troops still in China. He hands the document to Nationalist General Ho Ying-chin, the representative of Chiang Kai-shek. **November** - The Nationalists move their best divisions trained and equipped by the U.S. into Manchuria in what was to prove to be Chiang Kai-shek's biggest strategic mistake of the coming Civil War.

August 1945 - January 1946
Japan's surrender is quickly followed by a huge operation by the U.S. navy and air force to transport up to 500,000 Nationalist troops to formerly Japanese and Communist held parts of China. Most of the troops are transported to the northern and Manchurian ports from where they advance into the cities. At the same time the U.S. tries to broker a peace deal between the Nationalists and Communists in order to avoid a renewed civil war between the two parties. The Soviet occupation of Manchuria ends in November and Nationalist troops then take up their former positions. In the interim however the Soviet Army has handed over substantial Japanese arms and equipment to the Communists in Manchuria who still hold the countryside. In effect the Nationalists have taken the cities and towns of northern China but are surrounded by well-armed and well-motivated Communist forces. The stage is now set for the beginning of full-scale war between the Nationalists and Communists.

1946
January 13th - U.S. General George Marshal brokers a ceasefire between the Nationalists and Communists that neither side has any intention of honouring. **January 15th** - Even in the first few days of the ceasefire the Nationalists ignore the agreement and take the city of Mukden in Manchuria. **April** - Communists take Harbin and Changchun in Manchuria. **May 5th** - Nationalists Government return to Nanking. **May 19th** - Nationalists take Ssuping. **May 23rd** - Nationalists defeat the Communists in a battle near Changchun and re-take the city. **June** - U.S. negotiators arrange another short-lived truce between the two factions. **August 29th** - Nationalists capture Chengte. **August 30th** - USA agrees to sell large quantities of war surplus arms and equipment to Nationalists. **November** - Communists cross the frozen Sungari River to attack the Nationalists in their winter bases in Manchuria.

1947
January-March - Major Communist attacks against the 'elite' U.S. trained and equipped Nationalist divisions in Manchuria succeed in tying down these mobile units in static defensive positions. The morale of these better Nationalist divisions is sapped in futile attempts to keep contact between the various government held enclaves. This period sees three battles along the Sungari River - 1st Battle - January 5th to 16th, 2nd Battle - February 21st to March 5th and 3rd Battle - March 7th to 18th. **March 14th** - A morale boosting operation by 150,000 Nationalist troops and seventy-five aircraft takes the former HQ of the Communists at Yenan in Shensi province on the 19th. Although the victory gives the Nationalists a temporary boost the taking of Yenan is largely symbolic and has no real effect on the Communist war effort. **May** - Communist offensive led by Lin Piao with 270,000 men pushes the Nationalists back up to 150 miles and inflicts heavy casualties. **November 12th** - Communists take Shihchiachuang in Hopeh. **December** - Communist attacks cut all the rail links into Mukden and therefore isolate all the Nationalist held cities and garrisons in Manchuria.

1948

January 16th - First major Communist offensive in Manchuria. **April 2nd** - U.S. Congress agrees to aid the Nationalists and passes Aid Act. **May 23rd to October 19th** - *Siege of Changchun* - The Manchurian city defended by the 100,000 strong 'elite' Nationalist New 1st Army fell after a 150 day siege which saw a large number of civilian deaths from starvation. **June** - 200,000 Communists attack the Nationalist held city of Kaifeng defended by 250,000 troops. Although they briefly take the city they are driven out by the newly reinforced Nationalists who though victorious lose 90,000 troops. **August** - By the summer of 1948 the Communist North-East Field Army in Manchuria had fifty-four divisions with a total of 700,000 front line troops as well as 300,000 support troops. They faced a Nationalist force of 550,000 men in fourteen Corps and forty-four divisions including second line Peace Preservation Corps troops. **September 14th-24th** - Siege of Tsinan in Shantung Province. **October 5th 1948 to April 24th 1949** - *Taiyuan Campaign* - longstanding siege of the capital of Shansi Province held by 145,000 Nationalists against 300,000 Communists. When the city fell in April 1949 the defenders including hundreds of Japanese mercenaries were annihilated. **November 2nd** - Fall of Mukden in Manchuria. **November 5th 1948 to January 11th 1949** - *Huai-Hai Campaign* - This decisive battle of the civil war involved 920,000 Nationalist regular troops in seven armies against 600,000 Communist regulars. The Communists also had the support of hundreds of thousands of irregular volunteers who swung the balance in their favor. Strong Nationalist forces totalling 500,000 men were surrounded in the city of Hsuchow in Shantung Province by the Communists. Nationalist losses were over 300,000 with the majority being troops who chose to surrender to the Communists who also captured large amounts of U.S. supplied weaponry. Communist losses were also well over 100,000 men but this victory severely limited the Nationalists ability to defend Central China.

1949

January 1st - Nationalist Government offers to negotiate with Communists. **May 27th** - Fall of Shanghai to Communists. **October 1st** - Mao Tse-tung proclaims Peoples Republic of China in Peking and it now only remains to mop up the last Nationalist forces in Southern China. **October 15th** - Canton falls to Communists and Nationalist government is moved to the old wartime capital of Chungking in Szechuan Province in western China. **November 30th** - Fall of Chungking. **December 10th** - Nationalist leadership including Chiang Kai-shek withdraw to Taiwan. **December 25th** - Chengtu the last stronghold of the Nationalist government falls which effectively ends the Civil War. Remnants of the Nationalist Army withdraw into Burma and constitute the last anti-Communist troops on the mainland.

Manchuria 1931-1932

When the Japanese Kwangtung took over the three provinces of Manchuria in September 1931 they were faced by little organised Chinese resistance. On the orders of Chiang Kai-shek the Armies of Chang Hsueh-liang 'The Young Marshal' were ordered not to resist the Japanese and to withdraw in front of the invaders. Chiang's intention was that the Japanese would appear to the world as the aggressors and international pressure would be put to bear on them. This capitulation was not accepted by many of the Chinese soldiers in Manchuria and unofficial resistance to the Japanese began almost immediately. This tough looking Chinese soldier guarding an armoured train in 1931 is 'double armed' with both a Mauser C-96 pistol with wooden stock and a 'da-dao' fighting sword. His uniform consists of the peaked cap with high crown worn in the North of China and a padded jacket and trousers. It was men like this who made up the anti-Japanese volunteer armies which fought against the Japanese from 1931 without the support or 'official' backing of the Nationalist government.

This armoured train pictured in November 1931 in Manchuria is described in the caption as being used by the Anti Japanese Volunteer Army leader General Ma Chang Shan. After the defeat of the regular Chinese Army in Manchuria General Ma and other army officers refused to accept defeat and continued to fight the Japanese. General Ma made a personal declaration of war against the Japanese in September 1931 and continued his struggle into 1933. The various volunteer armies totalling well over 100,000 men, and reportedly up to 250,000 men, tied down thousands of Japanese and their Manchukuoan puppet troops for several years.

A young Nationalist soldier on patrol in Manchuria before the Japanese invasion in 1931 is wearing typical Northern Chinese soldiers uniform. The peaked cap is the pattern still being worn by the Northern Armies in the early-1930s and his jacket, trousers and puttees are in various shades of grey cotton. Interestingly he is armed with a Thompson M1928 sub-machine gun which may be a Chinese copy produced in one of the various Chinese arsenals. He has been issued with a canvas bandolier to hold spare magazines for the Thompson.

Young soldiers of the Nationalist Army are transported towards the front in Manchuria by train in late-1931. These men are well dressed and equipped for the fighting with fur hats and wadded cotton jackets and are armed with Japanese supplied Arisaka rifles. Although much of Manchuria had fallen to the Japanese during September resistance by regular and then irregular Chinese troops continued until the end of February 1932.

Soldiers of the White Sun

Taking cover behind a low brick embrasure these soldiers are waiting for a Japanese Imperial Army attack in the barren landscape of Manchuria in 1931. The hastily dug trenches offer limited protection from anything other than small arms fire and have no shelter for the men from the elements. Isolated positions like this were soon overrun by the Japanese during their conquest of the three provinces of Manchuria.

The Muslim General, Ma Chang Shan is pictured wearing his distinctive leather coat and fur hat during the period of his resistance to the Japanese. The General's refusal to give up his fight against the invading Japanese in 1931-1932 made him a "cause celebre" with both the Chinese people and the foreign press. He had already become a war hero by defending a vital bridge during the initial Japanese invasion. After his eventual defeat by the Japanese in 1932 he withdrew over the border into the Soviet Union. His return to China in the mid-1930s saw him take up various roles during the Sino-Japanese War.

After the withdrawal of the Nationalist Army from Manchuria in late-1931 these soldiers are manning trenches in new positions in February 1932. The men have at least been issued with fur lined winter hats which a few of them strangely have chosen to wear under their peaked caps. The padded and fur lined uniforms worn by the Northern Chinese troops were necessary in the bitterly cold winters of the North. It appears that this trench outside of a small town is defended with nothing heavier than the soldier's Mauser rifles.

Above: This machine gun team defending a trench in Northern China in early 1932 are armed exclusively with Japanese weaponry. The light machine gun is a Taisho Model 11 6.5mm that was made in Japan from 1922 and was already obsolete by the early-1930s. On the right of the photo the soldier is armed with an Arisaka Model 38 rifle which was standard issue with the Imperial Japanese Army. Arisaka's were used in the 1920s by some Northern Warlord troops who later joined the Nationalists and this could explain how it came in their use. Taisho 11s were not used by the Northern Armies however and this gun may have been captured from the Japanese.

Right: A column of troops march from the railway station to the frontline during the early fighting with the Japanese. The men have all been issued with standard winter uniform of fur hat and padded jacket and trousers. Equipment is very basic with only the two canvas bandoliers per soldier which have spare clips for their Mauser rifles.

Soldiers of the White Sun

Right: In this close up of two soldiers defending Manchuria against the Japanese invasion we can see the typical winter dress of the Chinese Army in 1932. Both men are wearing the quilted wadded cotton fur hat with the Nationalist sun emblem on the front. They also have padded winter coats and are fortunate to have been issued with woollen gloves as well. The Japanese influence on the pre-1928 Northern Chinese armies is shown by the fact that both men are armed with Arisaka rifles.

Below: Sword wielding soldiers of the Northern Chinese Army sit patiently in a shallow trench waiting to go into action in early-1932. They are wearing the typical Northern peaked cap with loosely sewn on cloth Nationalist sun emblems on their sleeves. This photograph's original caption reads, 'When the Orient Goes to War' and sums up how romantically the Western press viewed the idea of men fighting with swords against modern weaponry. The reality of course of any attack against dug in Japanese positions by these young soldiers would be far from romantic.

24

Manchuria, 1931-1932

A tough looking fighter of one of the Manchurian Anti-Japanese armies poses in the entrance to his hideout in 1932. Men like this were dismissed by the Japanese as bandits who had to be subdued before peace could be brought to the newly established state of Manchukuo. This man appears to be a leader of one of the volunteer units and is well armed with both a Mauser carbine and a Mauser C-96 'broom handle' pistol.

The original German caption to this photograph describes these Manchurian anti-Japanese volunteers in 1932 as 'bandit-soldiers'. As irregular fighters these men have to fend for themselves and find supplies wherever they can. They at least have managed to dress themselves in warm boots, overcoats and fur hats which are vital in the severe weather conditions of the Manchurian winter.

Soldiers of the White Sun

These pitifully armed anti-Japanese guerrillas pictured in October 1932 are volunteers of one of the armies which sprang up in Manchuria in the early-1930s. Their homemade spears would be of little use when up against the modern weaponry of the Japanese occupying army.

This French illustration of the early-1930s is a representation of the difference between the pre-1931 and post-1931 Chinese uniform. The officer on the left of the picture wears typical uniform of the Warlord period while the two soldiers on the right wear the Northern Chinese Army's dress. In the centre of the illustration is a soldier of the big sword troops fighting in North China in 1933.

After the Mukden Incident and the Japanese takeover of Manchuria in 1931-1932 the Chinese public in retaliation imposed an effective nationwide boycott of all Japanese goods and businesses. This boycott was very damaging to the already weak Japanese economy and in an attempt to break it by military means they landed troops at Shanghai in January 1932. Shanghai was the commercial centre of China and Japan's aggression against the city was meant to send a potent message to Chiang Kai-shek and his government. The city was defended by the Nationalist 19th Route Army who much to everyone's surprise put up a brave resistance to the 70,000 soldiers and marines of the Japanese invading force. After fighting which continued for over a month in the waterfront area of the port the Chinese Army had to withdraw from the city in early March. Due to the defeat by the Japanese the Chinese Government was pressured to officially abandon the boycott.

THE BATTLE FOR SHANGHAI JANUARY-MARCH 1932

A so-called 'Suicide Squad' is given orders before setting out on a mission in the region of Shanghai in 1932 armed with Mauser C-96 'broom handle' automatic pistols. The history of the Chinese Army of the early 20th Century is filled with 'dare to die' special units which were commando units invariably armed with pistols and fighting swords. In most cases the bravery of the Chinese soldier armed in such a fashion would not be of much use against Japanese machine guns.

A gun crew of the 19th Route Army operate an infantry gun during the fighting against the Japanese in Shanghai. The gun is a 75mm Infanteriegeschütz L/13 manufactured by the German firm of Rheinmetall and imported into China by the Dutch company HIH. This useful and compact artillery piece was light at only 375kg and could be towed into position by its crew which made it ideal for the Chinese Army. In 1932 the vast majority of the modern Chinese field guns were 75mm or smaller as the Nationalists had few vehicles to tow anything heavier.

Soldiers of the White Sun

Above: Young artillerymen of the 19th Route Army operate a battery of the L/13 infantry gun in support of their infantry comrades. The L/13 was a development of the German L/11.8 infantry gun that was also used by the Chinese during the 1930s. The gun crew may look young but they are tough veterans who have arrived in Shanghai fresh from defeating Communists in Kiangsi Province during the third encirclement campaign.

Left: Soldiers wait for the next Japanese attack in hastily dug firing positions during the battle for Shanghai. Most of the men are wearing the khaki woollen peaked cap and have their kit in their blanket rolls. They are fairly well equipped for Chinese soldiers and some have been issued with an entrenching tool. The officer in the centre of the group wears a ski cap and his armed with a Mauser Broomhandle pistol.

Opposite
Top: Firing from behind a barricade soldiers of the 19th Route Army in Shanghai in 1932 defend their position against the Japanese. The men of the 19th Army wore a mixture of field caps or in this case peaked caps with the KMT sun on the front. All are armed with the Hanyang Type 88 rifle which was a Chinese produced version of the German Gewehr 88.

Bottom: Soldiers of the 19th Route Army fire a Chinese manufactured Stokes mortar from behind a barricade of firewood. Mortars had been manufactured in China since the early-1920s and were a relatively easy weapon to produce. Sources say that they were made in a wide variety of calibres with the most common being 53mm, 60mm, 82mm, 120mm and 150mm. Most of the men here are wearing the pre-1937 peaked cap but the man in the foreground as an early type of field cap on.

The Battle for Shanghai, January-March 1932

Soldiers of the White Sun

The Battle for Shanghai, January-March 1932

Above: This defensive position near North Station Shanghai is manned by Nationalist soldiers. Armed with Hanyang Type 88 rifles and a Swiss made SIG KE7 light machine gun. The KE7 was a lightweight selective fire weapon that found its only export market in China and was not adopted by the Swiss Army. China was a ready market for any weaponry in the 1930s and the army found itself armed with some of the more obscure weapons being produced in European arms factories.

Opposite
Top: During the Fighting in Shanghai in 1932 a Browning M1917 machine gun crew fire their gun from a trench at the Japanese. The Browning manufactured in the U.S. was imported by the Chinese in their standard 7.92 mm calibre. Another version, the Colt-Browning Export model with spade instead of pistol grip was also imported by the Chinese in small numbers during the 1930s. Both crewmen have abandoned their equipment before going into their forward position although the firer has a civilian flashlight hanging from his shoulder.

Bottom: The same machine gun crew are seen a few seconds later with the firer flinching as he lets off his first rounds. Copies of the M1917 were manufactured in various Chinese arsenals during the 1930s including the Shanghai Arsenal. According to reports the quality of the M1917 copies were not too good as the original copy had been reverse engineered from a sample stolen from a Colt-Browning representative.

Troops fire their light machine guns from the shelter of a trench during the fighting around Shanghai. They are armed with the Swiss SIG KE7 and the man in the center of the group has leather pouches to carry spare magazines for his gun. Although the photograph is slightly out of focus we can see two different types of Chinese made helmet in use with this small unit. One is worn by the two men far left and right of the picture and is based on the plum blossom model worn by the Japanese in 1931-1932. The other two men wear a model of steel helmet which could be described as a primitive and larger version of the German 'coal scuttle' helmet. All of the soldiers' helmets have the Nationalist sun emblem stencilled on their left side.

Soldiers of the White Sun

Above

Left: This officer is firing his flare pistol from a command trench during the Shanghai fighting while the soldier in the foreground blows a signal on his bugle. The bugler is wearing the steel helmet peculiar to the Chinese Army of the period and from this picture it appears to have been quite crudely made. Although not like any other model of helmet in use with other armies it was in quite wide service in 1932 and was seen in small numbers as late as 1937. Perhaps it was designed and produced at one of the many small arsenals scattered around China at the time.

Right: During the 1932 fighting around Shanghai a Chinese defence line with a browning M1917 machine gun awaits a Japanese attack. The men wear wadded cotton jackets and early pattern field caps and in addition most have peasant's rain hats strapped to their backs. In contrast the officers directing their men's fire have green-khaki uniforms made of a woollen cloth with officer's grade field caps.

Left: General Tsai Ting-kai the commanding officer of the 19th Route Army is pictured in 1932 at the time of his units stubborn resistance to the Japanese in Shanghai. General Tsai was born in 1890 in Kwangtung Province and earned a reputation as a good officer when fighting the Communists and came to international prominence during the five weeks of fighting in Shanghai in 1932. In fact by holding out against several Japanese Divisions in the Chapei district of Shanghai, Tsai was ignoring Chiang Kai-shek's orders. After the withdrawal of the 19th Route Army the Nationalists signed an agreement with the Japanese which created a twenty mile zone around the city from which Chinese troops were excluded. The valiant stand taken by the 19th led to General Tsai becoming a national hero but his support for the Foochow revolt in late-1933/early-1934 meant he had to go in exile in Hong Kong. He was later accepted back into a command role in the Nationalist Army during the Sino-Japanese War and commanded the 16th Group Army.

The Battle for Shanghai, January-March 1932

Above: Firing from what appears to be a hastily dug entrenchment an anti-aircraft gunner uses his Oerlikon 20mm gun as a light artillery piece in the fighting of 1932. These Swiss light anti-aircraft guns and a cheaper Spanish copy by Hispano-Suiza were widely exported all over the world in the 1930s. They were often employed in the ground role especially when as in the case of the Chinese Army there was a shortage of conventional artillery.

Right: In the fighting of 1932 around Shanghai a Oerlikon 20mm anti-aircraft crew bring their gun into action against Japanese bombers. With no effective Chinese air force to counter the Japanese aircraft light anti-aircraft guns like this were the only weapons available to the defenders. The firer lies down on the ground to operate the gun so that he can get it to fire as near to vertical as possible. Although known universally as the Oerlikon the gun was actually originally a German design made by the Swiss firm of SEMAG and first sold to China in 1921.

Soldiers of the White Sun

The Battle for Shanghai, January–March 1932

Above
Left: In this crudely hand tinted postcard, a train of 'big sword' troops head for the frontline at Shanghai. The men appear to be armed only with their roughly made fighting swords which could be easily produced by local blacksmiths. Although better than nothing these swords would have been little use in modern warfare. The men are dressed in the usual grey cotton caps and jackets and have armbands which would carry a suitably patriotic message on them.

Right: This tinted photograph shows Nationalist troops of the 19th Route Army firing from their trenches. The soldiers are wearing the woollen green-khaki uniforms worn by some of the soldiers of the 19th Army. They are wearing their army issue blankets made into improvised packs by rolling their personal kit inside them and tying them at the ends. More men from the unit are take a break under the lean to shelter before taking their turn in the firing positions.

Opposite
Top: The gun crew of one of the large cannon of the Woosung Fortress which protected the mouth of the Yangtze and Whangpoo Rivers north of Shanghai bring their gun into action. During the battle for Shanghai the fortress shelled Japanese concentrations in the city as well as Imperial Naval vessels. At the same time the fort came under continuous heavy bombardment from the air and from the Japanese fleet. These bombardments put at Chinese estimates 50% of the fort out of commission by early February 1932.

Bottom: Another of the big guns in the Woosung Fortress is loaded by its crew who shelter behind its large shield during their bombardment of the Japanese Navy in early February. Although the main armament of the fort was destroyed the Chinese defence force constructed trench networks in the ruins of the fort and continued to hold back numerous Japanese infantry attacks. After the air and naval bombardment failed to take the fort the Japanese began to send in infantry attacks. During early February the fort was attacked by a 2,000 strong 4 Battalion Japanese Infantry force.

Right: During the Shanghai fighting a mortar crew fire their weapon towards the Japanese positions in the suburbs of the city. Mortars based on the British Stokes design were manufactured in several Chinese arsenals and came in several calibres. The crewmen are wearing grey cotton uniforms in this heavily tinted photograph with the peaked cap seen after 1932 only in use with the Northern Nationalist Army.

Above: Soldiers of the 19th Route Army line a trench and wait for a Japanese attack armed with nothing more than their Mauser rifles. Tinted photographs like this one are not always an accurate portrayal of the colours worn by the Nationalist Army. That being said most of the Chinese Army in 1932 were wearing the grey cotton uniforms seen here. As with the Nationalist Army in the late-1920s the officer wears a khaki cotton uniform in contrast to his men.

Soldiers of the White Sun

Bottom left: The same mortar crew is photographed from the rear with the loader steadying the tube while his officer checks his range. One big advantage for the Chinese Army when using mortars was they could be easily dismantled and moved to a new position by its crew. Manpower to move weapons like this was never a problem for the Nationalist Army but there was always a chronic shortage of vehicles to pull larger artillery pieces.

Above: In this tinted photograph a Maxim M1908 machine gun crew prepare to fire their weapon from a position in the undergrowth on the outskirts of Shanghai in 1932. Although getting the machine gun ready to attempt to shoot down low flying Japanese aircraft they have no anti-aircraft sights fitted. Maxims had been manufactured in large numbers in several Chinese arsenals since the Warlord Period and this could well be one of those home produced models.

Bottom right: A girl fighter from an unidentified volunteer unit fights alongside her male comrades in the trenches around Shanghai. She wears a side cap with her cotton jacket and trousers and has an identifying armband on her left sleeve. Her equipment consists of a leather belt from which hangs the bayonet for her Hanyang Type 88 rifle. The Japanese were no respecters of the fairer sex of China and if captured she could expect the same if not more severe treatment as her fellow soldiers.

After the takeover of Manchuria the Japanese laid claim to the Inner Mongolian Province of Jehol in the North-East of China in January 1933. Japan claimed Jehol as part of the new 'puppet' state of Manchukuo set up in the former Manchurian provinces. The Japanese invasion force was equipped with all the modern weaponry of war with a strong air force, artillery and tanks. They were faced by the poorly equipped Chinese local forces made up of the 4th, 5th and 6th Group Armies of the Nationalist Army. Assistance also came from the North-Eastern Loyal & Brave Army which was composed mainly of irregular cavalry. The defending forces had little or no heavy equipment and were to receive no assistance from the far off Chiang Kai-shek government. Although facing some resistance Japanese advances were only really held up by the Chinese winter and the fighting was over by March. After the end of the fighting A peace treaty of sorts was arranged and was signed at the end of May.

JAPANESE INVASION OF JEHOL 1933

'Wily' old General Tang Yu-lin poses on his horse for the Western Press outside his headquarters. A few months before in 1932 Tang had moved eight trucks full of his 'ill gotten' fortune which he had accumulated during his governorship of Jehol out of the province. When a Japanese invasion of Jehol seemed imminent he had sent his 'treasure' under guard to the Italian Settlement in Tientsin for safe keeping. Other reports say that the Japanese captured opium and other property which came to a value of $10,000,000 when they took the capital.

The military governor of Jehol Province, Tang Yu-lin with his bodyguard before the outbreak of fighting with the Japanese in January 1933. Although Tang had talked about "fighting to the last man" to defend Jehol when asked by Western journalists during the fighting about his armies situation he confessed that he "did not know where it was". He then deserted his troops and according to the press at the time was later executed by Chiang Kai-shek for this cowardly act. Tang was a former warlord who had treated the population of Jehol before 1933 badly and had even taxed "frying pans and water buckets".

Soldiers of the White Sun

Right: This group of bodyguards of Tang Yu-lin are all armed with the Czechoslovakian made ZH-29 automatic rifle. The Czechoslovakian ZH-29 was an advanced automatic rifle that was tested by several nations during the 1930s including the U.S. but was only purchased in small numbers by Ethiopia and China. ZH-29s were only seen in service with Northern Chinese armies and were probably bought independently by the local commanders like Tang Yu-lin themselves.

Below: In a rather picturesque and telling image from the campaign in Jehol these Chinese soldiers are defending a section of the Great Wall from behind sandbagged positions. Armed only with automatic pistols and rifles and exposed on top of the wall these men would be soon picked off by an attacking force. The conquest of Jehol by the Japanese took three months from January to March against brave but disorganised Chinese resistance.

Japanese Invasion of Jehol, 1933

Well turned out cavalry of the Chinese Army in Jehol parade before going into action against the invading Japanese Imperial Army. There were a large number of Cavalry units in the Armies defending Jehol with one Regiment and three Brigades in the 5th Army Group. In addition the volunteer 'North-Eastern Loyal & Brave Army' under the command of Feng Chan-hai was made up of three Cavalry Divisions and one Brigade. These cavalrymen have been well armed with Mauser rifles and wear a mixture of wadded cotton winter hats and fur lined hats.

In this newsreel still of the same defensive position as in the previous photograph a soldier looses off a round from his Mauser rifle. The man next to him has a fighting sword which equipped many Chinese soldiers in the early-1930s. All the men in this unit had been issued with padded coats and black fur lined hats and in this man's case a pair of thick winter gloves.

Sheltering behind a hastily dug fortification these soldiers wait for the advancing Japanese Imperial Army in Jehol in 1933. The men who include a soldier with a fighting sword strapped to his back and all of them are armed with Mauser rifles while in the centre of the group is a ZB-26 machine gunner.

Soldiers of the White Sun

A long column of troops advances across open country toward the Jehol front to engage the invading Japanese Imperial Army. The men are wearing various styles of cotton peak caps with some having a smaller and more relaxed crown which is similar in design to those worn by the Manchurian troops in the 1920s. Other men wear the standard shaped peaked cap which was the typical headgear of the Northern Chinese soldier before 1937. Their officer marching in the centre of the column wears a similar uniform to his men but in a lighter shade of grey.

A resolute looking 'swordsman' of the Chinese Nationalist Army poses against the brickwork of the Great Wall during fighting against the Japanese in 1933. His padded cotton jacket has an added fur collar and is worn with a locally produced winter hat with the KMT sun badge on the front. His 'Da-Dao' fighting sword may look brutal but would be lethal if he was able to get to close quarters with the enemy.

Soldiers of a 'Big Sword' unit pose for the cameramen wielding their large swords in the defence of Jehol province in 1933. The swords are based on the 'Ma-Tao' cavalry sabre used by Chinese warriors during the medieval period. These elite units were expected to go up against Japanese machine guns using 'cold steel' and if they were lucky, a broom-handle automatic pistol. Units armed with swords were a feature of Chinese Armies throughout the 1920s and 1930s and were often given the heroic title of 'do-or-die'. Although Nationalist propaganda in the 1930s extolled the virtues of these brave men the result of fighting machine guns with swords is not difficult to imagine.

Japanese Invasion of Jehol, 1933

This light anti-aircraft gun is operating during the Battle of Kailu during the invasion of Jehol Province. The strange looking gun is a British made, Vickers 1 inch gun which was sold in the 1920s as a ground and aircraft weapon and was installed in airships and on submarines. It should not be confused with the larger 1 pounder 'pom-pom' made famous during the Boer War of 1900-1902. How and why the Chinese Army acquired these guns is not known but they were just one of many 'exotic' types of light anti-aircraft gun in service. In fact it is safe to say that the Chinese used at least one of every model of this type of weapon available in the arms markets of the 1930s.

A young commando of the Chinese forces defending Jehol Province wears the winter padded cotton jacket and quilted winter field cap. He is armed to the teeth with his Mauser rifle as well as four stick grenades which he carries in canvas pouches on his chest. The grenades are modelled on the German type first used in the First World War and their crudely carved stick suggests that they were locally made in Chinese workshops.

Another soldier of the Jehol defending force is ready to go into action with his grenades strapped precariously to his chest. He appears to have simply tied cloth around the shaft of the grenades and then lashed them to together. Presumably he will unlash them before he comes into contact with the enemy as it could be a tricky procedure under fire. The jumble of ammunition pouches and spare clips for his rifle may not give him much of a military bearing but the fixed bayonet on his Mauser shows that he certainly means business.

41

Soldiers of the White Sun

Firing from behind a stonewall with hessian sacks stacked on top to give added protection as this soldier prepares for a Japanese attack in the mountains of Jehol. The cross stitching on his winter cap shows that extra quilting has been added to the standard issue hat and his ear flaps would be pulled down around his ears. We can also see that he has several canvas bandoliers full of ammunition for his rifle and he has his trusty sword ready for hand-to-hand fighting.

Soldiers manning a machine gun position in Jehol are wearing the usual heavily padded winter jackets. They also wear the fur lined winter hat seen only in use during the early-1930s in Manchuria and Jehol. The man on the right of the group has his ear flaps worn down while the officer on the left and another man in the centre wears theirs tied on top of their heads. Although not totally clear from this photograph the man firing the Czech ZB-26 machine gun appears to be wearing a steel helmet probably a British MK-I.

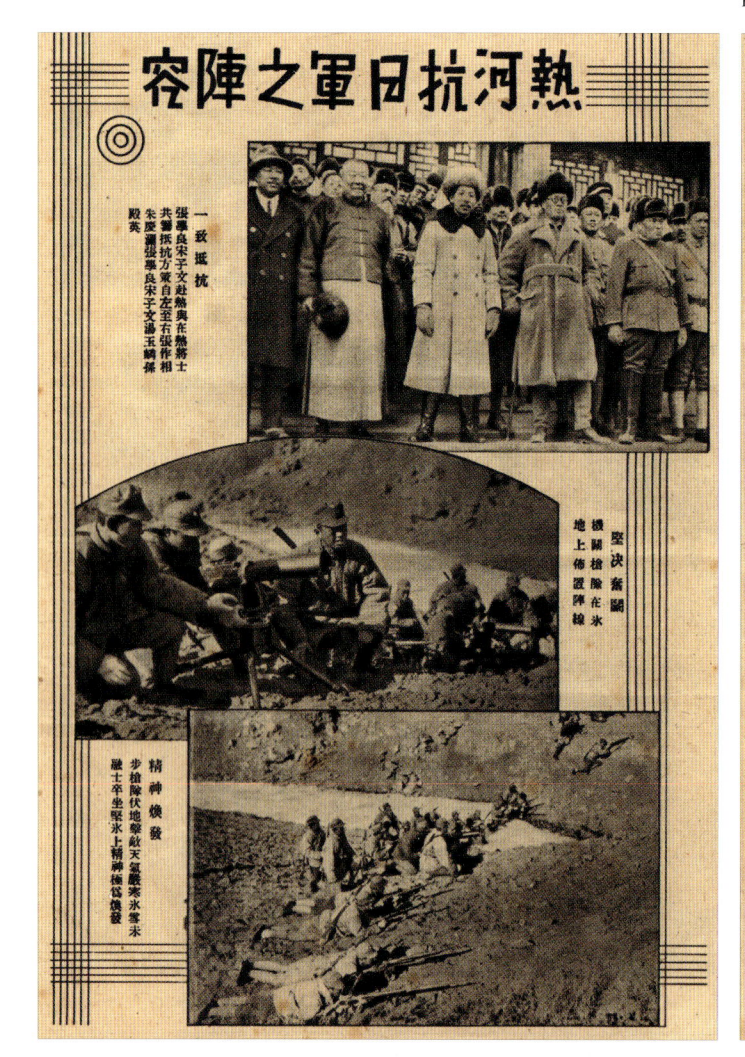

In a page from a Chinese news magazine of March 1933 the fighting in Jehol is shown in three photographs. The top photograph shows the commanding officers of the forces defending the Inner Mongolian province including on the right side, Tang Yu-lin. In the middle and bottom photographs the same machine gun team is featured as in the image from the front cover. The bottom image shows the badly exposed position of the gun crew defending a frozen riverbed.

This cover from a news magazine of 1933 shows a close up of A Browning M1917 machine gun crew. The Browning was one of the most popular machine guns in service with the Chinese throughout the 1931-1945 period. It was also one of the most copied models produced in the various Chinese arsenals from the 1920s. Chinese troops defending the province of Jehol had little heavy equipment and only a handful of machine guns to fight the Japanese with. They were poorly led and had poor organisation and could only offer token resistance to the invading army.

Japanese Invasion of Jehol, 1933

Above: General Fang Chen-wu and his staff during his armies campaign against the Japanese in Chahar Province in 1933. General Fang was a maverick who against Chiang Kai-shek's orders led his 20,000 men from Shansi province northwards into the contested province of Chahar. His so-called "Resist-Japan-Save-China Expeditionary Army" managed to recapture some towns in Chahar from the Japanese but his intended aim of liberating Manchuria were never going to be fulfilled. He had to sell his own property to finance his army and could get enough support to continue the struggle.

Above: Although not a good quality image this photograph of Chinese troops fighting near the Great Wall in 1933 does show the use of Soviet weapons. The men are armed with a Maxim M1910 heavy machine gun which could have been supplied from a variety of sources. It could have been given to the 'Christian Warlord' Feng Yu-hsiang in 1925 when he received Soviet support for a short period. Or it may have been one of the Manchurian Warlord Chang Tso-lin's purchases from escaping White Russians in the early-1920s. Official Soviet support for Chiang Kai-shek began in 1937 and arms were shipped in substantial quantities for the next four years. Between September 1937 and June 1941 the total amount of armaments supplied to China by the Soviet Union was, eighty-two tanks, 2,000 trucks, 1,140 artillery pieces, 10,000 machine guns, 50,000 rifles and two-million hand grenades. Ammunition supplied was made up of two-million artillery shells and 180 million bullets.

CIVIL CONFLICTS 1933-1936

The end of the fighting in Jehol and in the region of the Great Wall in 1933 did not bring any real respite to the Nationalist Government of Chiang Kai-shek. Chiang Kai-shek signed the Tangku Truce with the Japanese in late-1933 which was an agreement to demilitarise a large part of northern China near the Great Wall. This caused outrage amongst many patriotic Chinese and after the loss of Manchuria and Jehol to the Japanese was the final straw for former supporters of Chiang. The 19th Route Army's Fukien Rebellion of 1933-1934 was caused by what the rebels perceived was their punishment by Chiang of internal exile in Fukien far from their home region for having resisted the Japanese at Shanghai. Isolated rebellions like the one in Fukien had to be swiftly put down by the central government to allow Chiang to concentrate on his main concern. Chiang thought that the Japanese could not be defeated until the Communists in China were eliminated. He saw that the greater long term threat to his hold on power were not the Japanese who might keep 'nibbling away' at the outer regions of China until they were territorially satisfied, but the Reds. After the expulsion of the Communists from the Kuomintang in 1927 they had set up several military bases which had now become a threat to Chiang. A series of five large-scale extermination campaigns against these red bases were launched by the Nationalists from December 1930 until October 1934. These campaigns involved hundreds of thousands of troops and virtually the whole of the Nationalist Air Force. The extermination campaigns were aimed at destroying the largest Communist base in Kiangsi Province. Even though huge forces were committed to the first four campaigns they were largely unsuccessful in isolating the Red bases. By 1934 when the 5th and final campaign was launched the Nationalists were better organised and were in receipt of advice from the German military advisor General Von Seeckt and a team of his fellow countrymen.

Above: Hundreds of thousands of Nationalist troops were deployed during the Anti-Communist extermination campaigns of the early-1930s. Most were armed and equipped with the best that Chiang Kai-shek could provide and were usually far better equipped than their Communist foes. This Nationalist soldier on guard duty outside a barracks has not been so fortunate however. Although he has been issued with the full uniform of the regular Nationalist Army he has only managed to arm himself with a spear. He would of course presumably be given a rifle or other firearm as soon as any became available.

Right: Troops loyal to Chiang Kai-shek bring in prisoners from the rebellious 19th Route Army during the 'Fukien Rebellion' of 1933-1934. During this rebellion, soldiers of the 19th Route Army which had fought bravely against the Japanese in Shanghai in 1932 and then had been transferred to Fukien sided with rebels who formed an alternative Nationalist government in the city of Foochow. As with other rebellions of the 1930s the Fukien revolt was sparked off by its leaders view that Chiang Kai-shek was not standing up to the aggression of the Japanese. The rebellion was crushed by loyal Nationlist forces in January 1934 and its leaders went into exile in Hong Kong.

Above: Nationalist soldiers set out to take part in an 'extermination' campaign against the Communists during the early-1930s. The first four extermination campaigns from 1930 to 1933 were largely unsuccessful with heavy losses for the Nationalists. This photograph perhaps typifies the disorganised nature of the early anti-Communist campaigns with the rather ramshackle appearance of this patrol. In 1934 however the 5th Extermination Campaign succeeded in trapping the Communists in their Kwangsi base and forcing 100,000 of them to move thousands of miles to a new base in Yenan.

Right: Soldier manhandle a light mountain gun into position during one of the anti-Communist extermination campaigns of the early-1930s. All the men wear the rather strange looking stiff field cap which appears to have been based on the hat worn by the Nazi Brownshirts in Germany at the time. The five extermination campaigns between 1930 and 1934 involved the committing of hundreds of thousands of the best available Nationalist troops as well as much of the Chinese Nationalist Air Force. In Chiang Kai-shek's view the destruction of the 'enemy within' had to be completed before he could turn his attention to effective resistance to Japan's violations of Chinese territory in Northern China.

Soldiers of the White Sun

A soldier points out a target to the officer in charge of this machine gun crew during one of the extermination campaigns of the early-1930s. The machine gun is a Browning M1917 and can be identified as the model used by the U.S. Army rather than its export version because this one has a pistol grip. Belgium licensed produced the Browning and this machine gun could well be from the FN plant. Whether the gun came from the U.S. or Belgium it would have to made to take the 7.92mm ammunition which was standard in the Chinese Army.

This policeman on guard outside a government building in the early-1930s is well armed as befits his 'paramilitary' role. The police force under the Nationalist government in the 1930s and 1940s was expected to help to perform its normal role of dealing with criminals but also was expected when necessary to support the regular army. As well as criminals the police would try and keep a check on Communist activity and might be called upon to take part in local extermination campaigns He is armed with what appears to be a Hanyang Type 88 rifle and he is equipped with a Sam Brown belt and a small canvas bandolier.

The rather meek acceptance by Chiang Kai-shek's Nationalist Government of the Japanese demands for a demilitarised zone in North China caused outrage amongst many Chinese. There were a series of rebellions by soldiers in the region especially those affected directly by the imposition of the zone. Here on the 24th of July 1935 a civilian truck full of loyal troops are setting off to round up one of these protesting bands of rebels. Rebel soldiers were angry that the agreement with the Japanese meant that they were to be transferred without consultation to West China. They had seized an armoured train and attempted to storm the southern Yunting gate of Peking.

Civil Conflicts, 1933-1936

Right: These loyal troops are pictured on the same day as the previous photograph guarding the walls of the Southern gates of Yunting which were attacked by mutinous troops in July 1935. The original caption to the photograph says "Loyal Soldiers Greet Chinese Rebels with Shower of Bullets". Chinese people were totally divided by Chiang Kai-shek's policy towards Japanese encroachments on their territory. Opposition to Chiangs appeasement of the Japanese led to the Sian Incident of 1936 when some of his generals forced the Nationalist leader to form an uneasy 'united front' with the Communists against the invaders.

Below: Somewhere in the far North-West of China in the early-1930s a Nationalist unit marches past a rare automobile. This straggling column of troops is using bullock carts to transport their unit's heavy equipment. It was a constant struggle for the Nationalist government to maintain control over its vast tracts of territory especially in the outlying regions. The men are all armed with Mauser rifles and have been issued with padded cotton uniforms while the man at the rear of the group has a 'da-dao' fighting sword.

Soldiers of the White Sun

Above

Left: Soldiers of the Chinese forces facing the invasion of Suiyuan Province in 1936 wear new uniforms issued for the campaign. The men have padded cotton grey winter jacket and trousers on and a new type of peaked fur hat. These smartly turned out troops probably belong to an elite unit and do not really represent the majority of Chinese soldiers who fought in Suiyuan.

Right: Soldiers of a remote garrison in Suiyuan province in 1936 turn out for an inspection wearing the fur hats and padded clothing suitable for winter campaigning. The men have patriotic armbands and carry suitably emblazoned flags which proclaim their intention to defend their province from the Japanese and client troops from Inner Mongolia. All the men appear to be unarmed and the general shortage of rifles and especially heavier weaponry was particularly acute in remoter areas. The local commanders could expect little support from central government and had to rely on their own resources. During the fighting in Suiyuan in 1936 Chiang Kai-shek did however send 'special' anti-aircraft units to counter the Japanese planes loaned to the Inner Mongolians.

Right: During the fighting in Suiyuan Province in 1936 this Nationalist anti-aircraft machine gunner takes aim at attacking Japanese planes. He is firing a Type-24 heavy machine gun the Chinese produced version of the German Maxim M1908. This type became the standard model in use with the Chinese Army until the end of the Civil War in 1949. The campaign in Suiyuan was a relatively small scale affair with encroaching Japanese led Inner Mongolian separatists being roundly defeated by the Nationalists. When the Japanese opened a full scale offensive into China in 1937 Inner Mongolia and Suiyuan were swallowed up in the process.

Above: The caption to this photograph says, "little tank produced by China" it is however a French made Gnome & Rhone AX2. This 800cc motorcycle and sidecar was one of a number of such combinations used by the Chinese in the 1930s. These motorcycles with a small armoured shield and a ZB-26 machine gun were not really suitable for combat. If used in the reconnaissance role as in other armies they would have been a useful if rare addition to the small Chinese mechanised units.

Below: Well turned out Nationalist soldiers in Northern China in 1936 leave a parade ground after a military review. The men are all wearing either U.S. or British model steel helmets both types which were in service with the Chinese Army. They have full kit including knapsacks, canvas ammunition bandoliers and all have entrenching tools. Although the Chinese Army could always turn out a minority of its troops to this level unfortunately they could not equip the majority as well.

Soldiers of the White Sun

Above: Soldiers practice bayonet drill on the parade ground in the summer of 1936 as the Chinese Army prepares for the inevitable outbreak of war against the Japanese. All the men are wearing stiffened kepi type caps which were worn mainly by Northern troops before the Sino-Japanese War broke out. They are armed with what appear to be imported Belgian M1930 short rifles which were between a full sized rifle and a carbine. The photo caption describes the men as "Crack Troops of the Nanking Government" and their motor goggles suggest that they belong to a motorised unit.

Below: On a pre-war manoeuvre a gun crew shelter behind the large gun shield of their Bofors 75mm M1930 mountain howitzer. This modern Swedish made gun was one of the better artillery pieces in service with the Chinese in the 1930s. The gun crew who are just visible under the camouflage netting wearing British model steel helmets with their woollen khaki uniforms.

Japan's numerous provocations against the Chinese during the early and mid-1930s built up to the inevitable outbreak of full-scale war in July 1937. Japanese pressure on the Chinese Army in northern China had been building during 1937 and an incident in the region of the historic Marco Polo Bridge ignited the touch paper. The Japanese had abused their rights under the Boxer Protocol of 1900 to station up to 15,000 troops on Chinese soil. These substantial forces were much larger than those of the other foreign powers who had troops in China and far more than were allowed by the 1900 treaty. Effectively they acted as an army of occupation in large parts of the de-militarised north of China. Chinese units stationed in the region of the historic 17th Century Marco Polo Bridge southwest of Peking were attacked on the 7th of July. Japanese units in the area had been carrying out intensive military training near to Chinese positions and shots had been exchanged. In the meantime a Japanese soldier had failed to report back to his unit and his commander demanded to enter the town of Wanping to search for him. The Chinese commander in the region refused their demand and accused them of provocation. He said that the military exercises had been conducted without notice to his troops and this had led to the firefight. Attempted negotiations broke down and the Japanese attacked Chinese positions in the early hours of the 8th of July. The attack was repulsed by superior Chinese numbers and an uneasy truce was brokered which soon broke down. During the rest of July the fighting escalated and was followed by a Japanese attack on Peking at the end of the month and the attack on Shanghai in August.

THE OUTBREAK OF THE SINO-JAPANESE WAR 1937

A Hotchkiss M1914 medium machine gun crew of the Northern Chinese Army in the winter of 1936-1937 undergo drill. They are training to use their machine gun in preparation for any Japanese air attack in the build up to the second Sino-Japanese War. The man at the front of the machine gun holds the tripod steady while the other three fire the machine gun. All of the crew are wearing British pattern steel helmets and have padded cotton uniforms and have improvised backpacks made from rush matting.

Soldiers of the White Sun

Left: In this photograph dated February 1937 a mule drawn column of 75mm field guns advances towards an unspecified front. A few months later these guns would be defending China against the full scale invasion by the Japanese. Artillery was always in short supply in the Chinese Army with the average Division having about half the number of guns as in the equivalent Japanese Division. Those modern guns that were available were nearly always reserved for the Divisions that were loyal to Chiang Kai-shek.

Below: A ZB-26 light machine gun team prepare to defend their sandbagged emplacement on the Marco Polo Bridge near Peking in July 1937. An outbreak of fighting in the region of the famous bridge on the night 7th-8th of July began the full-scale war between China and Imperial Japan. These men belong to the 29th Army which was the main Chinese formation in the area when the Japanese attacked. The 29th Army was poorly equipped for the fighting with only rifles, fighting swords and a few machine guns.

The Outbreak of the Sino-Japanese War, 1937

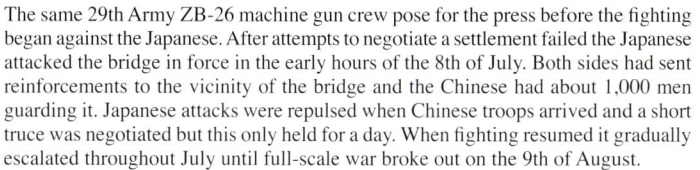

The same 29th Army ZB-26 machine gun crew pose for the press before the fighting began against the Japanese. After attempts to negotiate a settlement failed the Japanese attacked the bridge in force in the early hours of the 8th of July. Both sides had sent reinforcements to the vicinity of the bridge and the Chinese had about 1,000 men guarding it. Japanese attacks were repulsed when Chinese troops arrived and a short truce was negotiated but this only held for a day. When fighting resumed it gradually escalated throughout July until full-scale war broke out on the 9th of August.

A weary veteran of the 29th Army takes a break from the fighting near the Marco Polo Bridge with his broadsword at the ready. He is swathed in ammunition belts for a Maxim machine gun but the pouches on his belt suggest he is armed with a Mauser Broom Handle automatic pistol.

On the 7th of September 1937 a battle ready unit of the 29th Corps are seen on the march to engage the Japanese near Peking. These well-equipped troops include several who are armed with the famous fighting swords used especially by soldiers of the 29th. Several of the men have a row of four stick grenades dangling from straps over their shoulders and secured by tapes Their young officer has the equipment for the C-96 automatic pistol which he wears on his right hip with its wooden stock. The 29th Corps under the command of General Sun Che-yuan bore the brunt of the initial fighting against the Japanese.

Soldiers of the White Sun

The Outbreak of the Sino-Japanese War, 1937

Opposite
Top: Soldiers from the German trained Divisions of the Chinese Army are seen marching to reinforce their comrades attacking the Japanese at Loukouchiao. These men who are all equipped with the German M35 steel helmet were photographed on the 6th of August 1937 North of Peking near the Great Wall.

Bottom: Photographed in the middle of July 1937 a few days after the outbreak of the Sino-Japanese War these well turned out troops in their woollen uniforms look resolute. They are well armed with what appear to be ex-Japanese Arisaka 98 rifles and Czech ZB-26 light machine guns. Their kit includes blanket rolls as well as the canvas bandolier and the machine gunner in the centre of the group as a cleaning kit in a leather pouch on his belt.

This close up of a determined looking soldier of the Chinese Army near Peking shows a typical Northern soldier of the early war period. He wears a woollen peaked cap with the Nationalist sun emblem on the front and appears to be armed with a Japanese supplied Arisaka rifle.

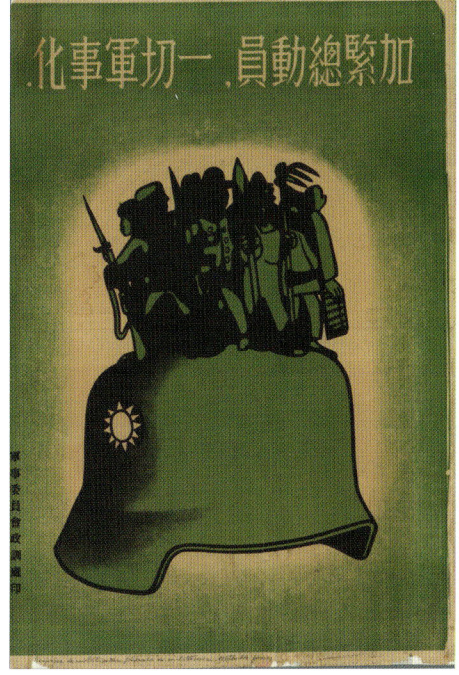

A column of soldiers descend from a section of the Great Wall in the days before the outbreak of the second Sino-Japanese War. The soldiers are wearing the British MKI steel helmet which was the main type worn by Nationalist units in Northern China. Although symbolically significant to the defence of China the reality was that any Nationalist units stationed along the wall would soon be destroyed by Japan's aerial superiority.

This 1937 poster uses the symbolism of a German helmet which was worn by many Chinese soldiers at the time. Stood on top of the helmet are the men of China military and civilian who could volunteer to fight the Japanese invaders. The caption at the top of the poster says 'Step Up General Mobilization, for Total Militarisation'

Soldiers of the White Sun

An artillery officer checks the range of his guns that are bombarding Japanese positions a few hundred yards away. The officer has camouflaged the range finder in an attempt not to give away his position to the enemy. He wears one of the many types of steel helmet in service with the Chinese Nationalist Army in 1937 and in this case it is the French Adrian M1915. As with its weaponry the Chinese Army imported steel helmets from several nations as well as producing copies of them.

Opposite

Top: Troops march off to the front through a apprehensive looking crowd during the first weeks of the Japanese invasion in 1937. The best Chinese Divisions were expended trying to take on the Japanese in conventional battles during the first months of the war and casualties were heavy. A conservative estimate was that from July to December the Chinese Army lost 124,130 killed and 243,232 wounded.

Bottom: Dug in on the banks of a canal a unit of soldiers wearing an early pattern Chinese helmet fashioned after the Japanese plum blossom model await an attack. This unusually shaped helmet is normally seen with a larger normal Nationalist sun insignia on the right side. A great variety of uniform types were seen being worn by the Nationalist Army in the early months of the 1937 fighting but most of the units wearing them were destroyed in the first year of the Sino-Japanese War.

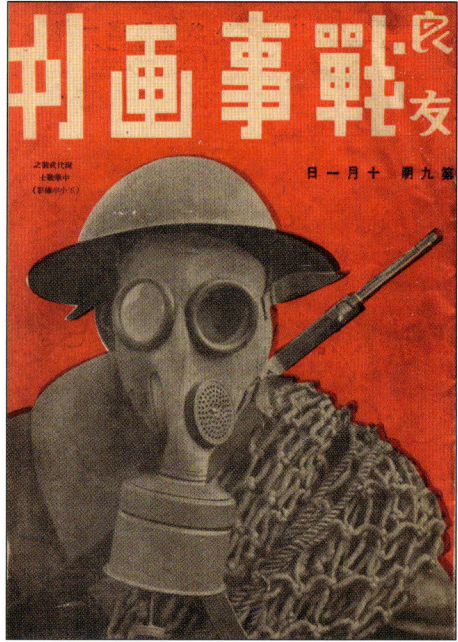

The rear cover of the Chinese published 'The War Pictorial' of 1st October 1937 shows a soldier kitted out with gas mask and British model steel helmet. He is armed with a 'Chiang Kai-shek' Mauser Kar.98k rifle and has camouflage netting slung over his shoulder.

This soldier armed with a Hanyang Type 88 rifle takes shelter in his own dug out and waits resolutely for the Japanese Army. The Hanyang was a copy of the German Gewehr M1888 and was one of the most popular rifles in service with the Nationalist Army.

The Outbreak of the Sino-Japanese War, 1937

Soldiers of the White Sun

Above: In a training area away from the Shanghai front in September 1937 a light anti-aircraft gun crew train on their German supplied 20mm. The gun is a Solothurn S5-106 which was imported by China in various models throughout the early and mid-1930s. China's anti-aircraft weaponry was made up mainly of a few hundred 20mm guns with a handful of larger calibre weapons.

Right: Searching the sky for incoming Japanese bombers this anti-aircraft gun crew prepare to fire their light gun. This gun is an Italian Canone-Mitragliera da 20/65 modello 35 Breda which was exported to China in 1935. Those Breda's that were supplied by Italy were reported in service only with three of the best trained Chinese Divisions in 1937, the 36th, 87th and 88th. Other Italian weaponry used by the Chinese included the 47mm Bohler anti-tank gun which was in service with the Nationalist 3rd Division. The Bohler had only just entered Italian service as the 47/32 model 35 when it was sold to Chiang Kai-shek in 1936. Italian supplies to China ceased with Mussolini's signing of the Anti-Comitern Pact with Japan. A ship full of Italian armaments was however reportedly on route to China when the pact with Japan was signed and the captain was told to wreck his vessel to avoid any embarrassment!

Above: Northern troops prepare to go into action against the Japanese near Peking in August 1937 fully expecting gas to be used against them. The men are wearing the standard model of gas mask which they would normally carry in the metal canister worn by the man in the centre foreground. Their arms and equipment are the usual Nationalist Army mixture with British MKI steel helmets, Mauser rifles that could have come from several countries and a Belgian automatic rifle.

Right: Sheltering behind a small hillock these soldiers are lucky enough to have been issued with gas masks. At this time in 1937 the Japanese were employing tear gas but a year later had started to use 'red' gas which made the victim feel very ill but without killing him. Probably through frustration at the Nationalists refusal to give up the fight the Japanese resorted to 'yellow' or mustard gas from 1939. Although gas was not universally used by the Japanese in China they used it on no less than 375 occasions during the Battle of Wuhan fought between August and October 1938.

Soldiers of the White Sun

Above

Left: Two officers demonstrate the French Mitrailleuse Hotchkiss de 13mm anti-aircraft gun in July 1937. The 13mm gun was described as an enlarged machine gun and could be used against ground targets but the Chinese bought some to use in the anti-aircraft role. As with weapons of its type it was far too expensive for its limited capability and only a few were imported by the Nationalists. Other light ant-aircraft guns used by the Chinese in small numbers in the 1930s included the Danish made 2cm Madsen Model 1935 and the Italian Canone-Mitragliera da 20/77 Scotti.

Right: China received a small number of modern German artillery pieces before the outbreak of the Sino-Japanese War. This FH18 105mm howitzer was as you might expect given to one of the divisions trained by German military advisors. The FH18 was the main medium field gun of the German Army and was the best that German industry could produce at the time. Unfortunately for the Nationalist Army those that were supplied were in such insignificant numbers that they could not make much of a difference. In total thirty-six FH18s were supplied to Nationalist China in 1936 and as far as is known this was the only delivery of this gun.

Opposite

Top: Artillerymen train pre-war with a piece of mountain artillery which is left over from the Republican Army of 1911-1928. The gun is a German made Rheinmetall 75mm M14 mountain gun which was imported by various armies during the early 20th century. All of the five-man gun crew wear the padded winter uniform with the firer having tightly wound cloth leggings with extra layers for the cold weather.

Bottom: The four-man crew of a German designed and Dutch produced under licence HIH 75mm L/13 infantry gun bring it into action. Three of the men put their weight on the legs of the gun to steady it while their comrades load their weapon. Presumably the lightweight of the L/13 which could be an advantage when transporting it meant that it was prone to be unstable when fired. The Chinese had a number of 'exotic' and little known guns in their armoury and these included several double purpose guns. These were normally arranged with two different calibre barrels e.g. 47mm and 81mm one above the other with one being used as a mortar and other as a conventional field gun.

Left: This poster is one of several issued at the time by the Chinese Government to urge its wounded soldiers to return to the front as quickly as possible. The poster is in the form of a storyboard which tells the tale of a soldier wounded, hospitalised but then going back to kill Japanese. Its four captions translate as, 'Wait Till My Wounds Have Healed, Then I'll Go Back to the Front'

The Outbreak of the Sino-Japanese War, 1937

Soldiers of the White Sun

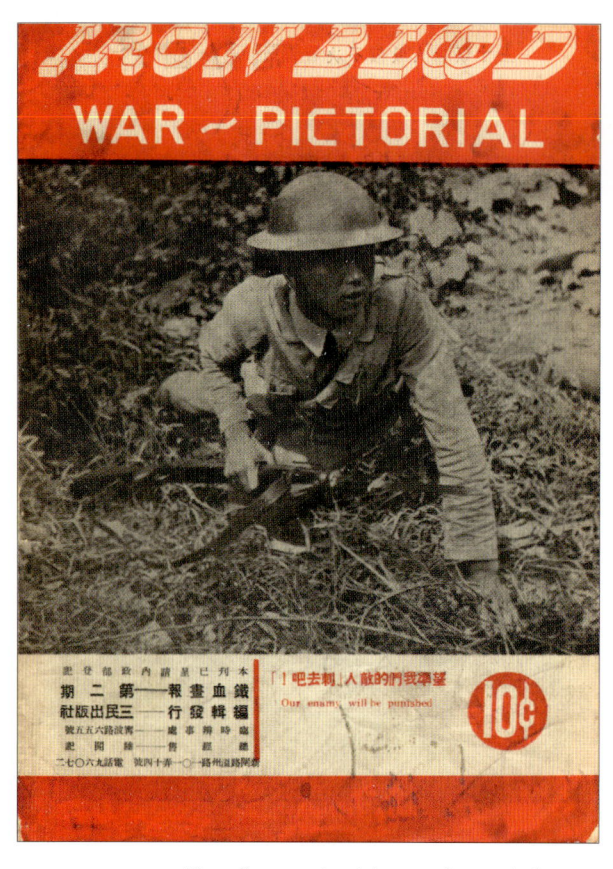

These four war pictorial covers show typical scenes of the Chinese Army during the first few months of the war against the Japanese. The magazines show soldiers advancing in camouflage, firing from trenches and readying a Browning machine gun for action during street fighting. Most magazines of this type carried patriotic slogans like the Iron Blood Pictorial that says, "Our Enemy Will Be Punished".

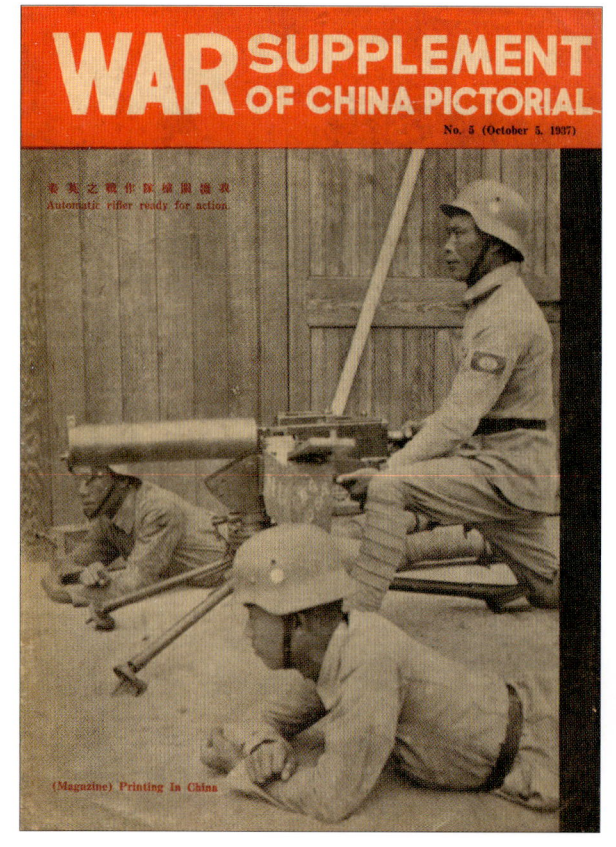

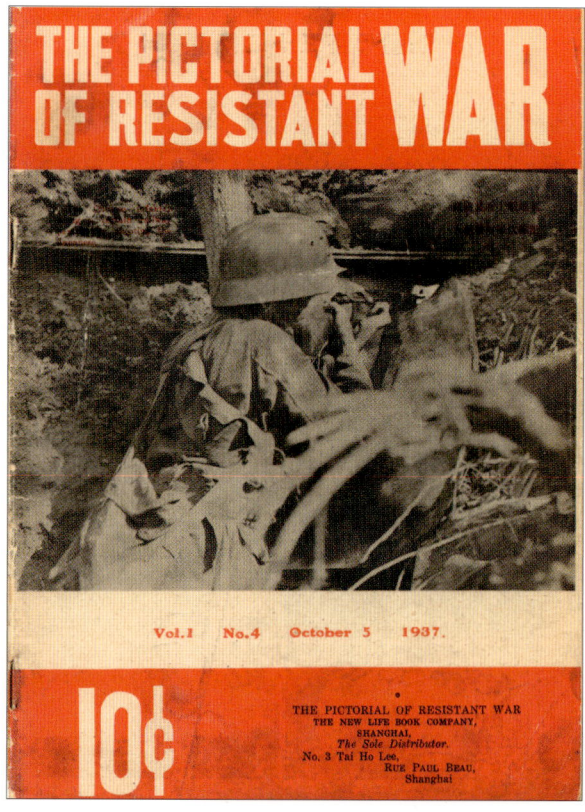

The decisive battle for Shanghai lasted from mid August until late October 1937 with much of the fighting taking the form of bitter 'house to house' fighting. In the first stage of the battle the Chinese launched aggressive attacks on the Japanese troops stationed in the centre of the city. This fighting which lasted from the 13th to the 22nd of August was followed by a series of Japanese amphibious landings along the coast around the city. Heavy fighting then ensued which lasted for two months and resulted in appalling casualties on both sides. During August-September and October the Japanese tried to overwhelm the Chinese defences in and around Shanghai in fighting that involved a total of nearly 1,000,000 men! Eventually the surviving Chinese withdrew from their positions and began a month long fighting retreat towards the Nationalist capital of Nanking. Chiang Kai-shek had lost many of his best-trained and equipped divisions in the battle but had proved that the Chinese were not going to give up the fight for their nation easily.

THE BATTLE FOR SHANGHAI AUGUST-OCTOBER 1937

On the approaches to Shanghai a young sentry stands in front of his sandbagged position while two men reinforce the strongpoint. Although we cannot see the Roman numerals on the soldier's unit patch it is probable that he belongs to the 88th Division. The defenders of Shanghai were reinforced by the 88th and 87th Divisions during the battle. Both Divisions had been trained and equipped by the Germans and were part of General Chang Chih-chung's 9th Army Group.

Two soldiers take up defensive positions behind a hastily built sandbagged position on the outskirts of Shanghai. Without adequate support these young soldiers could not hope to long resist the Japanese advance when it came. They are armed with German Gewehr 88 rifles or Chinese copies and each has a couple of largely empty canvas bandoliers worn over their shoulders.

Soldiers of the White Sun

Above: In this probably posed action shot a platoon of student volunteers rush towards the Japanese lines in the Shanghai fighting of 1937. The youth at the front of the group is a medic as is shown by his lack of weaponry and his red cross armband. All the volunteers have the British MKI helmet on and they are armed with the German Hanyang Type 88 carbine.

A lone girl sentry of the Citizen Training Corps stands guard over a trench in late September 1937. Young Chinese girls were to serve in a number of roles during the fighting in 1937-1938 and could expect little mercy from the Japanese. The way that the Imperial Japanese Army treated all Chinese civilians regardless of gender or age meant that female volunteers had a strong incentive to resist the invaders.

Young soldiers are about to literally 'go over the wire' during the early days of the fighting around Shanghai. These youths belong to one of the volunteer units raised by patriotic students to help the regular army defend China. Although the writing on the armbands they are wearing is unclear they would usually carry suitably patriotic texts proclaiming the wearers devotion to the defence of his country.

The Battle for Shanghai, August-October 1937

The front cover of the 1st of October 1937 issue of the Chinese illustrated magazine 'The War Pictorial' shows a Hotchkiss M1914 medium machine gun crew. Both crewmen wear the U.S. or British pattern steel helmet with their light khaki canvas uniforms. They are firing their French made machine gun from a gun pit camouflaged with netting and foliage.

A lone soldier fires his Mauser Kar.98k rifle towards the advancing Japanese from behind a hastily constructed barricade of undergrowth. Chiang Kai-shek's plan for the battle for Shanghai was to use some of his best troops to confine the Japanese to a limited front. This plan was totally undermined when Japanese forces were landed behind his troops defensive positions in November.

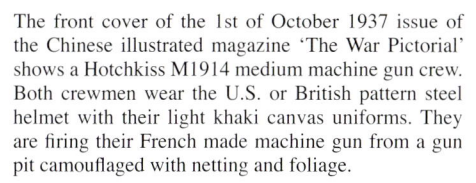

An officer and one of his men stand on top of a Chinese bunker constructed as part of the defences of Shanghai. The battle for Shanghai was complicated by the fact that the city contained several foreign concessions. These French and the International concessions were neutral zones which both the Chinese and Japanese recognised. Military contingents from several nations guarded the concessions and this bunker could be a few hundred yards from a British or French held guard post.

The original caption to this photograph says that this assault boat on the Shanghai Front in September 1937 is full of Engineer troops. Although there is a Browning Model 1917 machine gun at the front of the boat to give covering fire the men would be an easy target for the Japanese on the opposite bank of the river. All the crew wear the unique Chinese steel helmet worn by some units on the Shanghai Front. This model helmet was not based on any foreign makes and appears to have been designed in China and produced in small numbers.

Soldiers of the White Sun

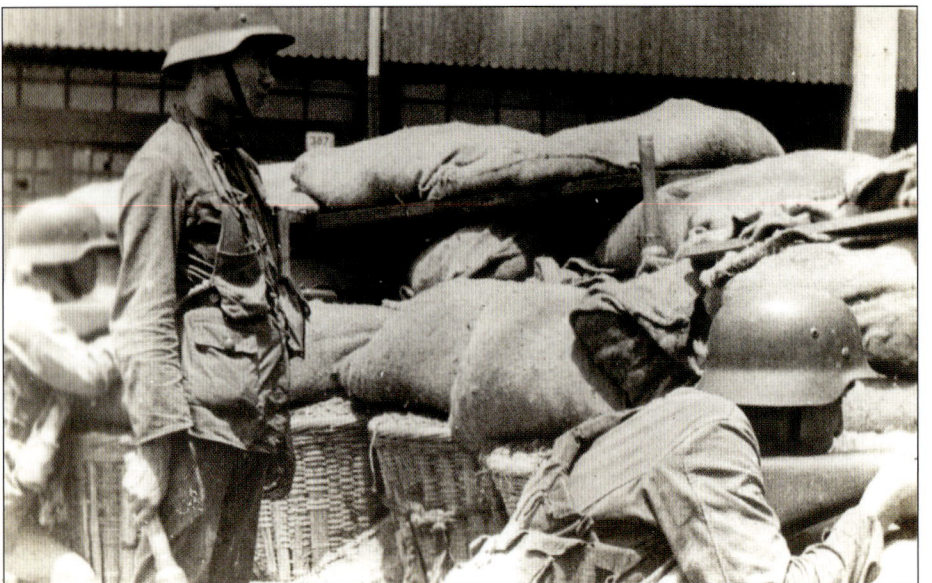

Left: Young volunteers move through a farmer's field near Shanghai during the first weeks of the Japanese attack against China in the summer of 1937. These volunteer units were soon bloodied in the fighting in 1937 and 1938 when any hopes of the Chinese Army throwing the Japanese out of their country were soon dashed.

Opposite
Top left: A young soldier of the 88th Division steadies himself as he fires off a few rounds from behind a sandbagged strongpoint. The 88th Division is the one most identified with the battle for Shanghai but eventually there were thirty-three Divisions in nine Army Groups involved in the struggle. The soldier is wearing a typical light khaki cotton shirt and shorts with puttees and M35 helmet. He is well equipped with a water bottle, canvas bread bag and canvas bandoliers to carry bullets for his Hanyang Type 88 rifle. His comrade to his left has a Chinese umbrella on his back which may have been issued to him or brought with him from home.

Top right: This soldier posing outside the sandbagged position he is defending is wearing a woollen khaki uniform with his M35 helmet. Most soldiers defending Shanghai wore a lighter khaki cotton uniform and this soldier maybe from an elite bodyguard unit. The only equipment he has is a water bottle, a flashlight and the canvas holdall to carry his German made stick grenades.

Bottom: The same soldier as pictured in the previous photograph is photographed here with his unit's young mascot. Boy soldiers were often attached to Chinese units but this youngster looks a little small to be a combat soldier. He has been kitted out with a specially fitted uniform and wears an adult Sam Brown belt which dwarfs him.

Left: Three soldiers prepare to throw their stick grenades from their sandbagged position towards the Japanese in the bitter fighting for Shanghai. The youthful faces of the two soldiers in the foreground are partly obscured by their arms as they try and gain impetus for their grenades. Both youths now have an empty pouch in their grenade bandoliers and will have to wait for the erratic supply system to get replacements. More and more Chinese troops were sucked into the fighting for Shanghai where Chiang Kai-shek hoped to break the Japanese Army's will.

Left: By the end of the long and bitter struggle for Shanghai both sides were exhausted but the Chinese had particularly suffered. By October 20th the Nationalist Army had lost about 130,000 men in the fighting in which although numerically stronger they were totally outgunned by the Japanese. The Chinese forces around Shanghai were eventually forced to withdraw when large Japanese forces were landed by sea on the 10th of November. The landings of four Japanese Divisions at Fushon, South of Shanghai and at Chiang-yin to the North would have quickly led to the encirclement of the Chinese troops. In order to try and save some of the best Nationalist Divisions the Chinese had to make a hasty retreat before the jaws of the trap were sprung.

The Battle for Shanghai, August-October 1937

Soldiers of the White Sun

Right: General Wang Ching-chiu, commander of the 87th Division studies the sky in case of Japanese air attack on the 1st of October 1937. General Wang's troops had been stationed in the campus of Shanghai University since August and continued to hold their positions throughout the fighting for the city. Wang was to be given higher command during the war and by the Winter of 1944 he was commander of the 10th Army Group.

Far right: The cover of the Chinese published magazine 'War Supplement Of China Pictorial' dated the 17th of October 1937 is captioned " Just tossing a hand grenade to check the invading forces". This young soldier is typical of the German trained and equipped divisions that bore the brunt of the Japanese invasion. His equipment is however all Chinese with the canvas bandoliers around his chest and waist with German type 'potato masher' hand grenades tucked into them.

Below: A rare piece of Chinese medium artillery fires from a wooded position during the 1937 fighting. The gun appears to be a Austro-Hungarian 75mm M11 which was imported into China before the First World War. This field gun would have probably served in various Chinese Warlord armies before being taken over by the Nationalists in 1928.

The Battle for Shanghai, August-October 1937

Another pre-1914 artillery piece of the Chinese Army is brought into action in the fighting for Shanghai. Its crew pose very formally for the camera as if on parade rather than in the midst of a battle. The chronic shortages of medium and heavy artillery in the Chinese Army were never really addressed even with the advent of U.S. military aid after 1941.

A Flak 30 anti-aircraft gun crew train to use their gun in the ground role in an attempt to make up for the army's shortage of conventional artillery. The Flak 30 could be used as an anti-tank or anti-personnel gun and an AP40 round was issued to the German Army for the former role. It is doubtful however that the Chinese bought this type of gun to use in any other role than the anti-aircraft one. It is not known if they had much if any of the special ammunition needed for the gun to be used in the ground role. Presumably the German advisors who recommended that they buy the Flak 30 would have alerted them to its capabilities.

This cover of the October 9th 1937 issue of the war supplement of the China Pictorial magazine shows a medium artillery piece in action. The 75mm field gun is one of a small number of artillery pieces in service with the Chinese in 1937. Most of the heavier equipment of the Chinese Army was lost during the early months of the Sino-Japanese War. Those that remained were kept mainly in the hands of Chiang Kai-shek's more trusted Divisions on whose loyalty he could depend.

Captain Liu seen stood in front of a PAK35/36 anti-tank gun was the commander of an 'elite' motorised detachment. The detachment was made up of a battery of PAK 35/36 anti-tank guns towed by German Kfz 15-Horch Medium cars. The guns was escorted into battle on the Shanghai Front in 1937 by German Zundapp K800 motorcycle side-car combinations armed with ZB-26 machine guns.

69

Soldiers of the White Sun

Top left: This re-touched photograph shows an officer as he stops to examine a Mauser C-96 automatic pistol he has found to go with the one he has tucked into his belt. A surreal touch is added to the scene as the officer is stood at the side of a sign pointing to the 10th Tee of the Shanghai golf course

Above: This dramatic poster from 1937 shows the gigantic figure of a Chinese soldier stood astride the ruins of a town. The caption extols its reader to make sacrifices for the fatherland saying, 'Swear to Defend the Nation to the Death'.

Left: In a piece of pure propaganda, two soldiers near Shanghai are shown for the press holding a flag which is supposed to belong to Manchukuoan soldiers fighting for the Japanese. The flag however appears to be a doctored Japanese rising sun flag which has added stripes to the normally plain white field. Although puppet Manchukoan soldiers were employed by the Japanese in North China in 1937 their unreliability meant that they were kept well away from the battle fronts. Manchukuoan troops were used after 1937 by the Japanese to perform occupation duties again mainly in Northern China.

The Battle for Shanghai, August-October 1937

A student volunteer mans his trench armed with a Hanyang Type 88 rifle which was a Chinese made copy of the German Gew M1888. During the first months of the Sino-Japanese War many patriotic students came forward and volunteered to fight. Conscription of students by the Chinese government did not officially begin until July 1939 when certain 'specified' groups were recruited. These were usually students who were studying subjects such as medicine which made them particularly useful to the war effort.

This Chinese cartoon of October 1937 features ghostly Nationalist soldiers looming over the Great Wall of China is captioned simply, "To Defend Our Fatherland". During the first months of the war against Japan the defiant spirit of the Chinese people was evident in propaganda such as this.

A heavily camouflaged Chinese Type 24 heavy machine gun with accompanying riflemen armed with Mauser rifles prepare to hold their ground. The crewman feeding the ammo belts in from the right hand side of the Type 24 is barely visible under camouflage netting.

Two student soldiers wait with bayonets fixed in the undergrowth around the University of Shanghai for a Japanese attack. These young patriotic volunteers were widely featured in Chinese propaganda during the fighting for Shanghai. With little heavy weaponry available to the Chinese defenders the battle for Shanghai was always a one sided affair.

Soldiers of the White Sun

Above: This well equipped Chinese soldier is pictured on the cover of the October 5th 1937 issue of an illustrated supplement of the war pictorial paper. Unlike most Nationalist soldiers of the period who were light equipped he has a full canvas pack and has his bayonet fixed to his Mauser Kar.98k rifle. The caption on the front of the magazine grandly states "Chinese defenders fighting for their National Defence as well as international peace".

Right: A machine gunner firing a French Hotchkiss M1914 tries to shoot down one of the 270 Japanese aircraft flying against the Chinese during the Battle for Shanghai. The Chinese air force had committed themselves up to 140 of their precious aircraft to the battle and these included a mix of types of planes that came mainly from the U.S. and Italy. The machine gunner who is armed with a C-96 Broom Handle pistol is able to operate the Hotchkiss by himself as the bullets are on 249 round strip belts instead of the normal metal strips. A standard metal strip for the Hotchkiss held either 24 or 30 rounds and was ideally fed into the gun from the left by a second crewman.

Above: In this candid photograph soldiers grab a quick meal of rice at the side of the road before returning to the fighting. The age of the soldiers varies but it is noteworthy how young many of them are and some look in their mid teens. They nearly all have M35 steel helmets and the youth in the foreground has his Mauser 'Chiang Kai-shek' rifle beside him.

Right: A close up of a soldier in a front line position shows his Mauser C-96 automatic pistol to good effect. The C-96 was so popular with Chinese armies throughout the 1920s and 1930s and was imported by the many thousands. This insatiable demand for the C96 led to foreign arms manufacturers especially in Spain making copies in large numbers and exporting them to China. One company in the Basque region of Spain produced a copy of the Mauser which was adapted to suit the Chinese liking for rapid-fire weapons. This adaptation meant that the gun could be fired on full automatic which emptied the ten round clip in less than a second. Because of the lightness of the gun this not only left the firer having to fit a new clip but meant that the pistol jumped around in his hands and could not be fired with any accuracy!

Right: During the street fighting in Shanghai a ZB-26 machine gunner uses his weapon to fire at the Japanese aircraft bombing his position. The Chinese chose well when they bought the first ZB-26s from Czechoslovakia in 1928 and it was to serve them throughout most of the period covered by this book. Known in Chinese service as the Type 26 it was manufactured in several local arsenals and served alongside the Canadian produced Bren until 1949.

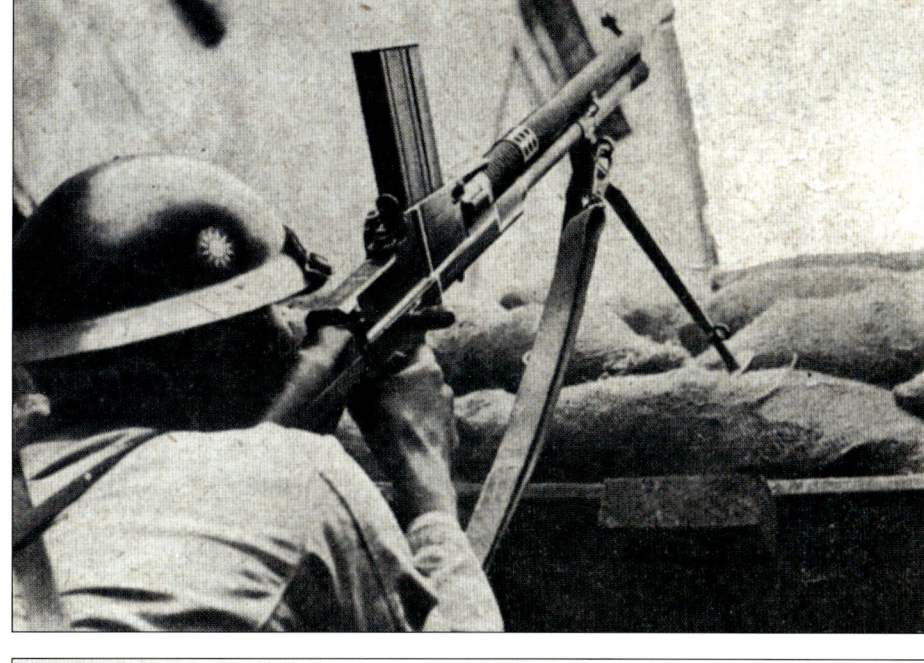

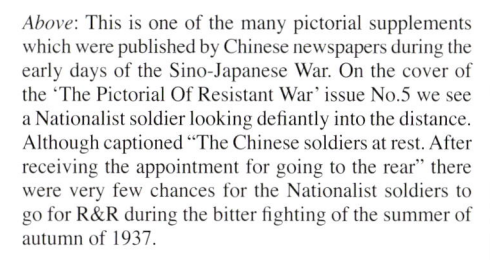

Above: This is one of the many pictorial supplements which were published by Chinese newspapers during the early days of the Sino-Japanese War. On the cover of the 'The Pictorial Of Resistant War' issue No.5 we see a Nationalist soldier looking defiantly into the distance. Although captioned "The Chinese soldiers at rest. After receiving the appointment for going to the rear" there were very few chances for the Nationalist soldiers to go for R&R during the bitter fighting of the summer of autumn of 1937.

Right: Sitting on a grassy bank this ZB-26 machine gunner raises his gun skywards in a probably vain attempt to shoot down the Japanese planes attacking his position. Without the aid of the gun's bipod stand to steady his aim this kind of shooting would rarely be successful. The soldier is a smartly turned out private from one of the German trained divisions defending Shanghai in 1937.

Soldiers of the White Sun

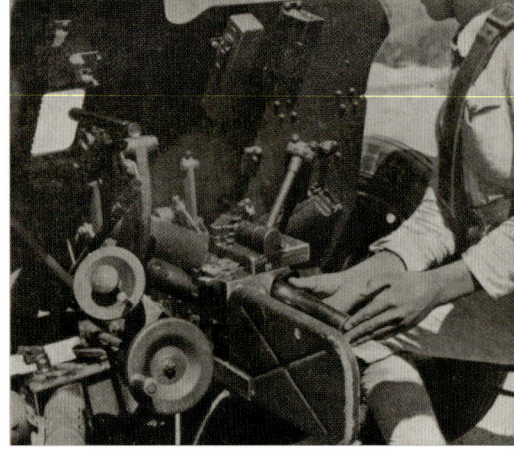

Above

Left: The crew of a PAK 36 3.7cm German anti-tank gun bring their weapon into use in the fighting of 1937. These modern guns were in front line service with the Germans until well into World War II so for once the Chinese had some up to date artillery. PAK 36s were more than capable with dealing with the thinly armoured Japanese tanks in service in China. *Right*: In this close-up a trainee undergoes training with a PAK 35/36 37mm anti-tank gun before going into action. The few modern guns like this were concentrated in the hands of the German trained Divisions who were most loyal to Chiang Kai-shek. Although the PAK 35/36 was capable of dealing with all the lightly armoured Japanese tanks there were simply not enough of them available to the Chinese in 1937. Japan's heaviest tank in 1937, the Type 89 had a maximum armour thickness of 17mm and the PAK35/36 could penetrate up to 49mm of armour at 400 yards range.

Right: The famous news cameraman H.S. Wong, known internationally as "Newsreel Wong" was the only Chinese journalist operating in this field before World War II. In a typical scene Wong is pictured by another newsman at the frontline during the fighting in Shanghai in 1937. His newsreels for MGM were shown all over the world and helped highlight the plight of China during the 1930s. Perhaps his most famous photograph is one taken of a baby alone wounded and crying on Shanghai railway station seconds after its mother has been killed by Japanese bombs.

Right: The caption to this photograph reads, "Chinese Broadsword Corps Forward to enemy's battle positions". During the fighting in 1937 large numbers of sword wielding Chinese soldiers were photographed for the international press. How practical a charge of soldiers with broadswords was against a Japanese machine gun can be imagined.

The Battle for Shanghai, August–October 1937

Left: This assault platoon of soldiers waiting to go into action against the Japanese during the early days of the war appear to have taken the fighting sword to another level. They seem to be armed with wooden staves with curved blades fastened to the top of them giving them the appearance of medieval halberds. Unfortunately the quality of the photo does not allow for detailed examination of these primitive weapons. As well as the bladed weapons the men are liberally armed with egg grenades instead of the more common stick version.

Above: On the back cover of a war pictorial magazine from 1937 we see the rear view of a 'big sword' soldier advancing. He is wields his 'da-dao' fighting sword in menacing manner but is also well armed with a Mauser C-96 automatic pistol. His equipment is complete with a brown leather cartridge belt around his waist which carries spare magazines for his Mauser. Tucked into the back of his belt is the wooden removable stock for the C-96 which gave the pistol its nickname of 'broom handle'.

Left: A student volunteer fires his rifle at advancing Japanese Imperial Army troops from behind the shelter of a tree. The soldier's canvas bandoliers appear to be largely empty which does not bode well for any sustained firefight with the enemy.

75

Soldiers of the White Sun

Above: A commanding officer of a unit of the 88th Infantry Division examines a map of his defence lines with his junior officers. All the officers' uniforms appear to be devoid of all ranks and insignia and this may be for security reasons. The Nationalist Army suffered devastating losses of 10,000 of their junior officers during the battle. This left only about 15,000 of the junior officers who had been trained at the Central Military Academy from 1929 to 1937 still available to Chiang Kai-shek.

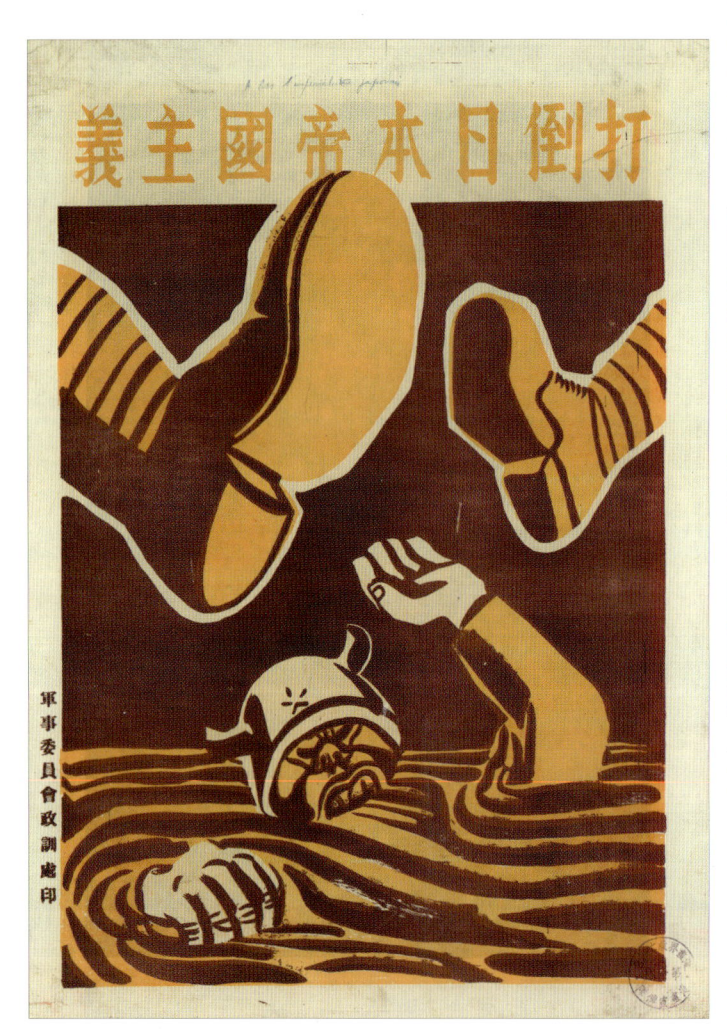

Above: A U.S. bubble gun card illustrates the story of the 'Doomed Battalion' of Shanghai which held out in a warehouse it had fortified for several days against Japanese assaults. Under the leadership of Colonel Hsia Ching-yuan the battalion fought bravely against the repeated Japanese attacks. When their position became untenable Colonel Hsia led his men through one of the holes in the warehouse wall. He had noticed that the four Japanese machine guns were aiming at his men's escape route all fired simultaneously. This meant that when they ran out of ammunition there were a few seconds when his men could escape without being shot at. Using this method nearly all his men were able to escape to internment in the British International Settlement unscathed.

Above: Exhausted soldiers from the 'Doomed Battalion' rest under the curious gaze of British troops from the International Settlement where they have been interned in November 1937. These men are the lucky ones as any captured Chinese troops would usually be immediately executed by the Japanese. It was not till later in the war that the Japanese spared some Chinese troops if they were willing to fight in 'puppet' units.

Above: In this 1937 Nationalist poster the boots of Chinese soldiers push the horned and evil Japanese soldier symbolically into the river. The racist tone of the poster was matched by those issued by the other Allied powers who portrayed 'buck toothed' Japanese. Its message is simple and is contained in the caption which says 'Defeat Japanese Imperialism'.

The three photographs on this page show one of the most numerous types of tank in service with the Chinese at the outbreak of the Sino-Japanese War, the Cardon-Lloyd VCL. The VCL was a British made light amphibious tank made in 1931 and was too lightly armoured to be used effectively in the combat role. In total the Chinese government bought twenty-nine of these vehicles and they served with the 1st Armoured Battalion in Shanghai. The first photograph shows a column of VCL's with turrets reversed and the second shows one on manoeuvres. In the third photograph we can see the unit insignia on the sides of the turrets and the final photograph sees a unit of VCL's on parade.

Soldiers of the White Sun

Left: A crew of a Rheinmetall Panzerabwehr- Kanone 35/36 L/45 37mm anti-tank gun pose in the Shanghai region. The number of the 37mm PAK 35/36 supplied to China are not known exactly but the best estimates say that around 125 were supplied between 1936 and 1938.

Above: A rare mechanised unit on the road to the frontline is made up of motorcycles and a German supplied Kfz-11-Horch 830 medium car. These command cars came in various models and were supplied to China to act in their primary role but were also useful to tow their 37mm anti-tank guns.

Left: This illustration from the cover of a supplement of an Italian newspaper is dated 28th of November 1937. It shows the Chinese Army retreating headlong in front of the Japanese advance towards the Chinese capital of Nanking and is indicative of how many in the world saw the fighting. Although Italy was not formally aligned with Japan at this time the Fascist press's sympathies appear to have been with that nation. It was only a year or so before this that China had a 140 man strong Italian training mission for its air force. They had also been supplied with 100 combat planes including the latest Italian fighters and bombers. Italy also supplied the Chinese with several types of anti-tank and light anti-aircraft guns in the mid-1930s.

The autumn and winter of 1937 see further defeats for the withdrawing Chinese Army with the fall of most of the country's major cities. Japanese advances into Inner Mongolia and Shansi province in the northwest bring even more territory under their control. At the same time their major victories in battles in the East of China lead to the fall of the Chinese capital of Nanking. Events at the fall of Nanking stun the outside world with the brutality of the Japanese Army reaching unparalleled levels. Atrocities in Nanking bring sympathy from Europe and the United States and fail as intended to force Chiang Kai-shek to negotiate. China's military losses during this period are extremely heavy with 367,000 men killed from July to December as well as most of the army's modern equipment.

CHINA'S AGONY CONTINUES OCTOBER–DECEMBER 1937

Above: Well camouflaged against low level Japanese air attacks a precious Bofors 75mm M29 anti-aircraft gun and its crew hide from the Japanese on the outskirts of Nanking on the 13th of October 1937. The anti-aircraft defence of Nanking was undertaken jointly by the Air Defence School, the Cadet Regiment of the Ministry of War and volunteers from the Central Military Academy. If Chinese government sources are to be believed the 75mm guns protecting Nanking accounted for one enemy aircraft for every 300 rounds fired.

Top right: This mobile searchlight is taking part in pre-war manoeuvres to test the governments anti-aircraft capabilities. As with all branches of the Nationalist Army in 1937 there were always small quantities of modern anti-aircraft equipment available to protect a few big cities. Unfortunately there were never enough searchlights and guns and many towns and cities went virtually unprotected.

Right: This 75mm Bofors M29 crew are operating their gun against daytime attacks on Nanking in 1937. The M29 was a popular weapon with many of the worlds armies in the 1930s as it was a relatively easy to operate. It did not necessarily need complicated fire-control systems as used by similar guns from other countries and so was ideal for nations with limited resources.

Soldiers of the White Sun

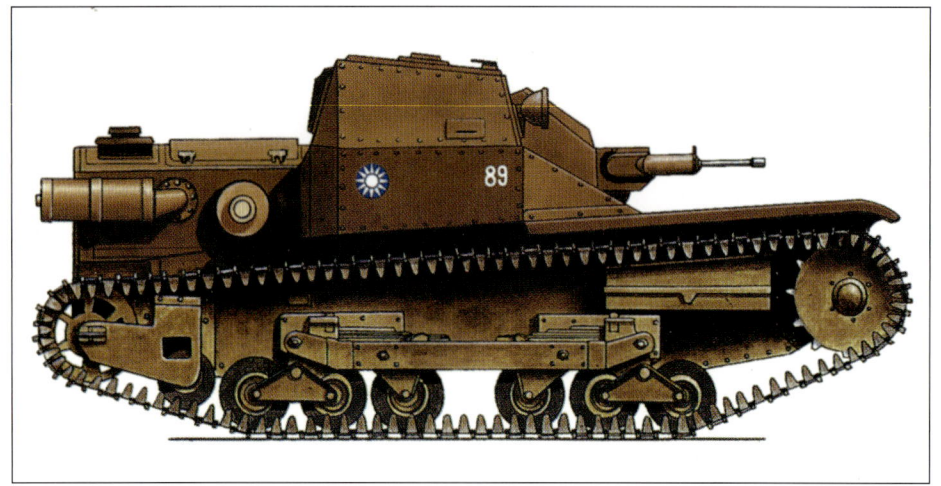

Above: This Italian made CV-33 tankette or light tank is finished in brown khaki overall with the Nationalist sun badge stencilled on the side. The CV-33 provided a number of smaller or poorer armies including the Chinese with a cheap alternative to conventional tanks. As the Italians were to find out in North Africa in 1940 the CV-33 had limited combat worth. With a limited armament of two Breda 8mm machine guns and its light armour the CV-33 was not worthy of the name 'tank'.

Above: On the cover of a Chinese pictorial magazine of October 1937 a British made Vickers 6-ton Type 'E' tank is seen in action in "rugged terrain". The 6-ton tank with its 47mm main armament was imported into China in 1936 and was used in the following year's campaign against the Japanese. Most of the sixteen Type 'E' tanks were knocked out during that year and several were captured by the Imperial Army

Left: German supplied PzKpfw.I Sd.Kfz.101 Ausf.A light tanks along with Italian CV-33s and a few armoured cars made up the 3rd Tank Battalion of the Chinese Army. The 3rd Battalion fought during the battle for Nanking and lost all of its Panzer I's to the Japanese. Numerous photographs exist of Japanese soldiers posing in front of captured vehicles that had been employed piece-meal by the Chinese. This vehicle has machine guns as its main armament and was intended as a reconnaissance tank rather than a main battle tank. The tank's insignia was limited to a vehicle number on the front and the Nationalist sun emblem on its side.

Left: A Chinese artillery crew fire their field gun from a dug in position during the 1937 fighting. The crew all are dressed in winter wadded cotton jackets and trousers worn with the standard field cap and have backpacks improvised from a rolled up blanket to hold their kit. Unusually two of the crew at least have Thompson M1928 sub-machine guns with the twenty round box magazine. Chinese artillery crewmen would not usually be this well armed and would in fact be lucky to have any side arm at all.

Right: This Swedish Bofors 75mm M1930 mountain howitzer was one of seventy-two purchased by the Chinese government. According to the records the guns had originally been intended for sale to Turkey but China took over the order when the Turks could not finance the deal. Chinese agents were renowned for ordering weapons and equipment from numerous arms manufacturers. Of course this policy meant that weaponry was not standardised within the Chinese Army and replacements and ammunition were often difficult to obtain.

Right: Two officers peer from an exposed position towards the enemy positions that their men are firing at from the relative shelter of a trench. The junior ranks of Nationalist officers suffered terrible casualties during the first few years of the war. During the heavy fighting for Shanghai and Nanking during 1937-1938 it is estimated that the Army lost 10,000 junior officers as well as hundreds of thousands of their best recruits. Because the soldiers of the better Divisions lost in 1937-1938 were seen as officer material this meant that the Army lost most of its potential leaders. These heavy losses were to effect the performance of the Nationalist Army until its final defeat by the Communists in 1949.

Right: These two armoured cars used in the defence of Hangchow are based on the peerless car of First World War vintage. With their domed turrets armed with twin Maxim heavy machine guns these armoured cars should have been a match for very similar vehicles in service with the Japanese in 1937. Unfortunately the Chinese did not have the numbers of armoured vehicles to match the Imperial Army and Navy's.

Soldiers of the White Sun

The four photographs on this page and the next all show young women volunteers who fought alongside the men at the front from 1932-1937. Women were allowed to serve in a number of military organisations with the Citizens Training Corps being the most prominent. All the young women in the photographs wear the same floppy caps and loose fitting cotton jacket and trousers which were typical volunteer uniforms. In three of the photographs the volunteers are armed with Chinese produced Hanyang Type 88 rifles which were rather cumbersome for the slight oriental frame.

China's Agony Continues, October-December 1937

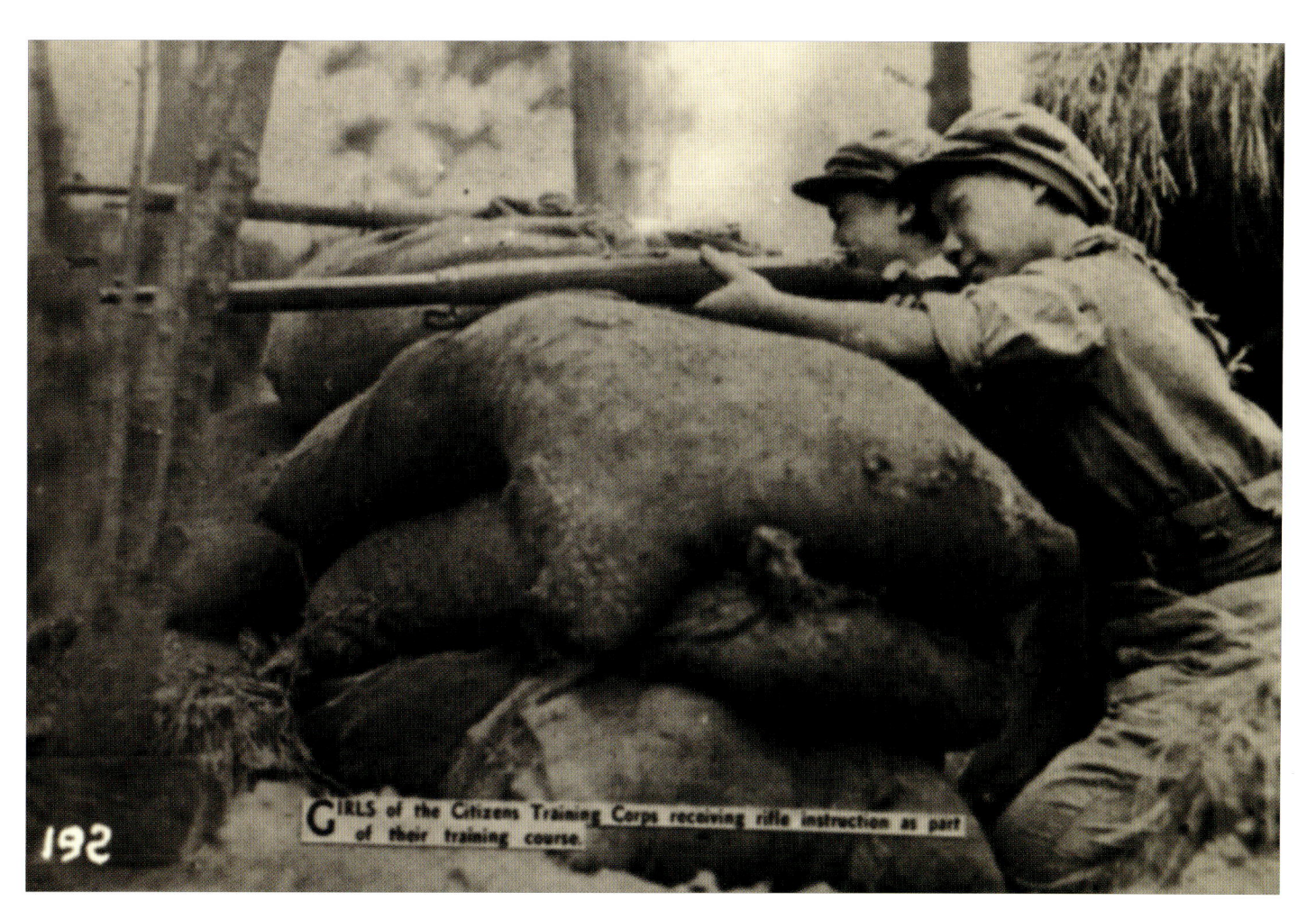

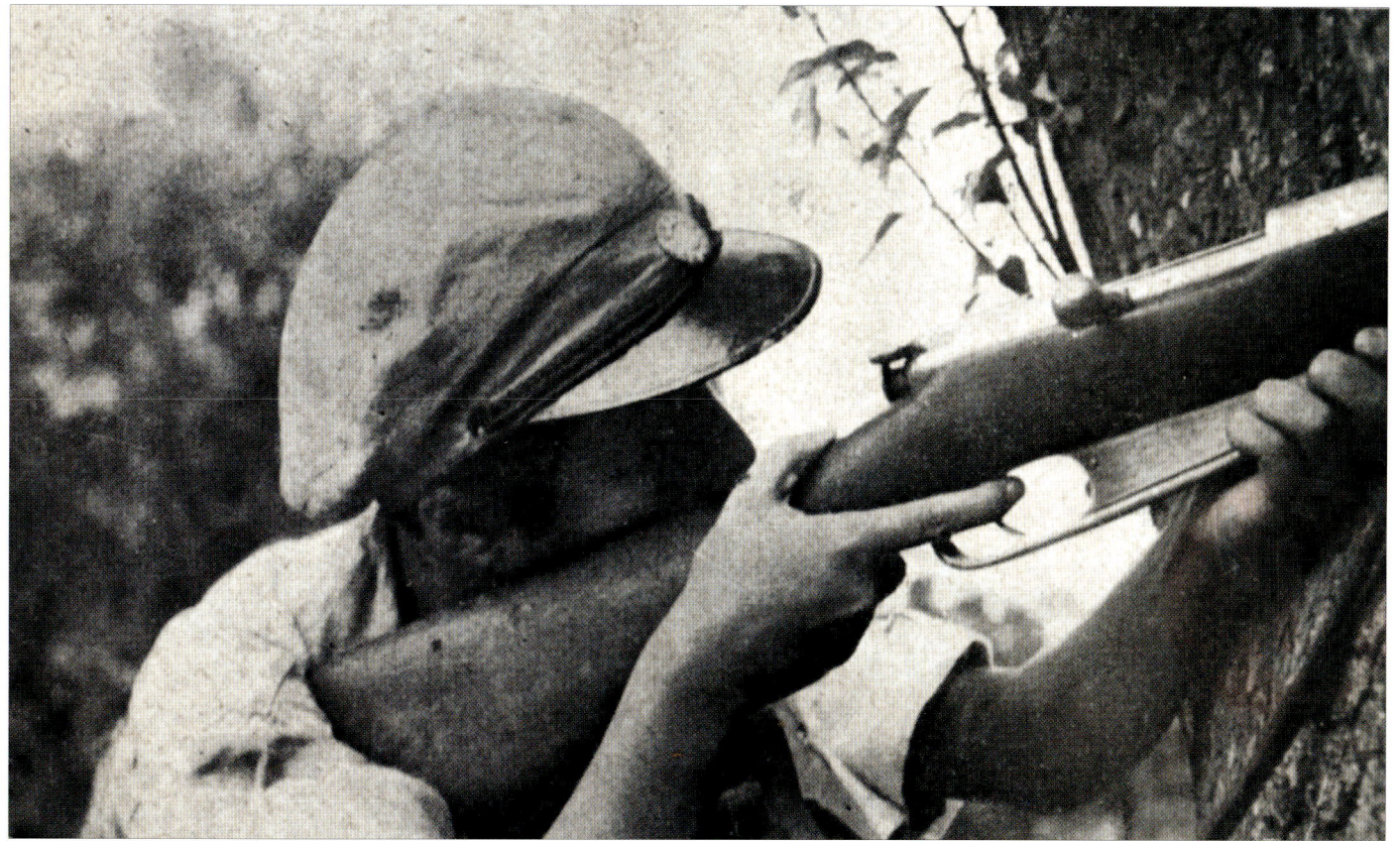

GIRLS of the Citizens Training Corps receiving rifle instruction as part of their training course.

Soldiers of the White Sun

Left: In this storyboard type poster from 1937 has the captions, 'No Compromise, No Surrender, Fighting to the End, for the Ultimate Victory'. The pictures convey the same message with the fighting soldier, tearing up any peace overtures offered by the Japanese and standing proudly for final victory.

Above: This photograph purports to show captured armed militiamen and a woman who are being paraded for the cameras by Japanese soldiers. Presumably the poor devils are to be executed afterwards by their captors who stand grinning behind them. The scene appears however to be even more sinister than first appears as it looks as if the Japanese have simply slung a Hanyang Type 88 rifle over the bewildered girls neck for effect. Any chances of meaningful co-operation by the Chinese population with the Japanese were ruined by the inhuman treatment meted out by the Imperial Army.

Left: This young militiaman is part of a group of civilians who have volunteered to fighting alongside their regular army comrades during the first few weeks of the war. Soldiers of the regular Nationalist Chinese Army were routinely executed when captured by the Japanese so this youth could expect no mercy from them. Although wearing civilian clothes this volunteer has managed to acquire a rifle and a single stick grenade and a canvas bandolier as used by his regular comrades.

Right: The members of a village self defence group stands waiting for inspection before going into action against the advancing Japanese Imperial Army in 1937. Regular Chinese soldiers were treated brutally by the Japanese if captured so these men and boys can expect no mercy from their enemy. They are mostly armed with elderly Mauser M1871 rifles which were supplied to the Imperial Chinese Army in the late 19th century.

Above: A smiling girl guerrilla fighter is armed to the teeth with her C-96 automatic pistol with spare magazines in the pouches around her waist. She also has a grenade hung rather precariously around her shoulder on a piece of string.

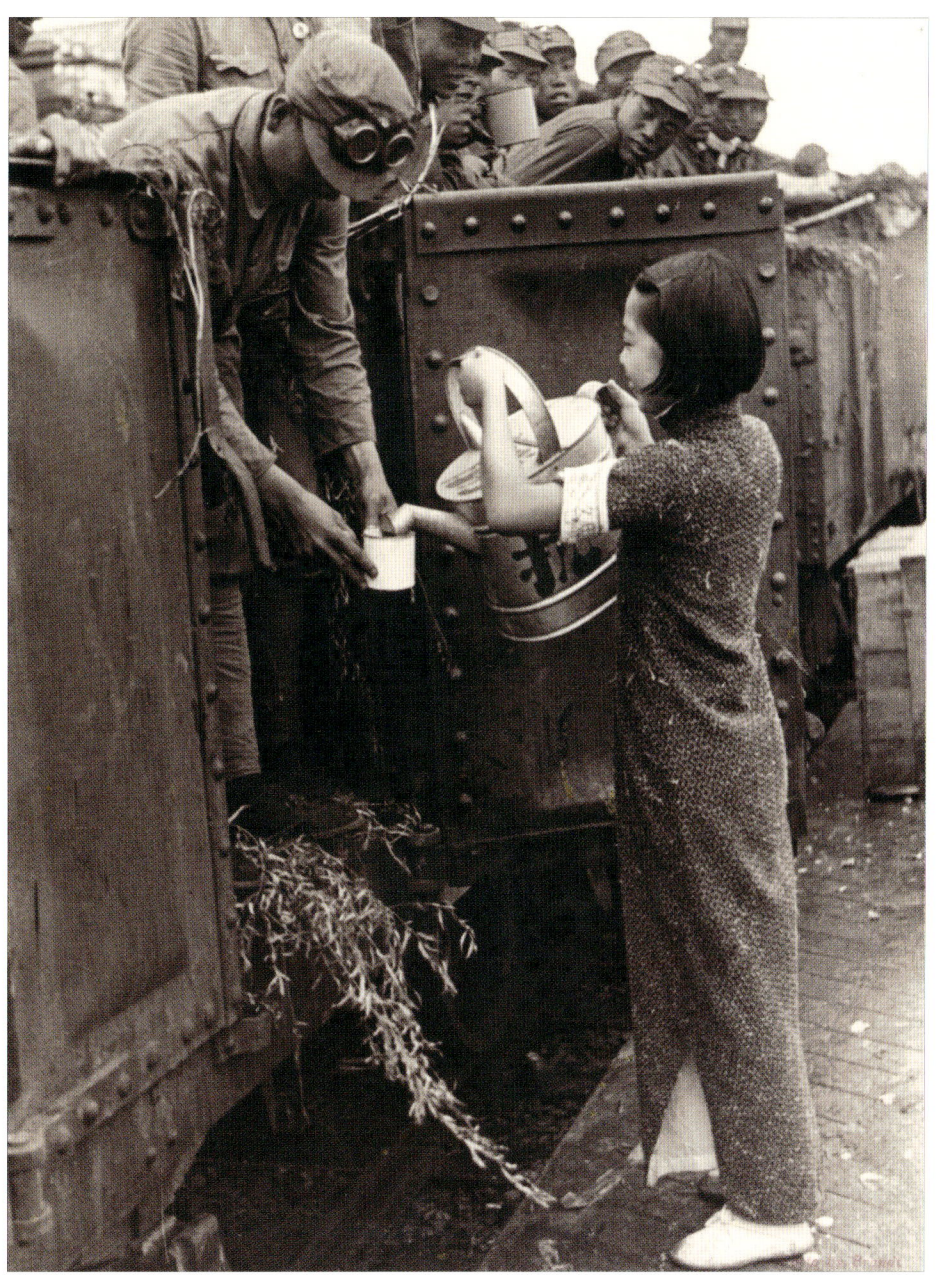

Right: A young woman volunteer serves tea to troops being transported to the frontline by rail during the first year of the Sino-Japanese War. Throughout the war against Japan the women of China had a major role in supporting their men folk in the army.

Soldiers of the White Sun

Right: An exultant Chinese soldier stands with his foot on the neck of a dead Japanese invader in this 1937 poster. The posters caption proclaims that the Chinese nation has to resist for it to exist and says, 'If There's an Enemy, I can't Exist, if I'm there, the Enemy will be Vanquished'.

Below
Left: A primitive patriotic matchbox cover shows a rare piece of heavy Chinese artillery firing at the Japanese.

Right: Another patriotic matchbox cover features a Maxim machine gunner who 'bravely' fires his gun while shells explode around him.

Over three long years from 1938 until the beginning of the Pacific War and Japan's attack on Pearl Harbour in December 1941 the Chinese stood alone against the Japanese. With little outside military aid available after the cut-off of German arms shipments only the Soviet Union supplied substantial amounts of armaments during 1938. The Japanese Imperial Army continued to conquer more territory during 1938 with the coastal cities of Foochow, Amoy and Swatow falling in May and Canton and Wuhan falling in October. In March 1939 the Japanese took the city of Nanchang and invaded Kwangsi province in November. 1940 saw the formation of a 'puppet' Chinese government in Nanking as the Japanese tried to 'divide and rule' their newly conquered territories. In the period just before Pearl Harbour the Japanese continued to try and consolidate their hold on the areas of China they controlled. Although the fighting in China had abated slightly by 1941 the Nationalist Army continued to resist the Japanese Army's offensives. China's military losses during this period were terrible with between 1938 and 1941 the army losing 1,322,175 killed. The number of wounded was slightly higher for the same period with estimates of 1,333,787 reported. Bearing in mind the almost complete lack of medical care for the ordinary Chinese soldier many of the wounded would have died.

CHINA'S CONTINUED RESISTANCE 1938-1941

Muslim troops of the Chinese Army are pictured in this 1938 photograph which has the original caption, 'The Sons of the prophet are brave men and bold'. These troops were first raised from amongst the Muslim population of Shantung province to fight the Communists on their border. By 1938 they were fighting the Japanese in Hopei and were considered to be some of Chiang Kai-shek's more reliable troops. Their officer wears the same basic uniform as his men and has the ammunition pouches for a Mauser C-96 automatic pistol around his waist. His men are very basically equipped with simple canvas bandoliers and they are poorly armed with a number of different rifles. These include a Russian Mosin-Nagant M1891 and an Austrian Mannlicher M1886 which could have seen service with the pre-1911 Chinese Imperial Army.

Soldiers of the White Sun

Left: This U.S. bubble gum card from the 'Horrors of War' series shows a march through Hankow of the Kwangsi Women's Battalion on the 10th of January 1938. The battalion of 150 women fighters had arrived in the city after a 600 mile march with fifty pound packs and armed with Mauser rifles and had been hand picked from amongst thousands of volunteers. Their marches through cities threatened by the Japanese advance with drum beating and flags flying were intended to stir patriotism in the men and encourage them to join the army.

Above: Fleeing Japanese soldiers are loomed over by the avenging figure of a Nationalist soldier in this 1938 poster. The slogan reads, "The Longer We Fight, the Stronger We Become. The Longer Our Enemy Fights, the Weaker They Become".

Left: An officer directs the fire of his Model 53 - VZ-37 machine gun crew at a low flying Japanese aircraft during fighting in the Summer of 1938. The Czechoslovakian made VZ-37 was imported in some numbers into China during the 1930s along with the VZ-26.

Left: The crew of a German supplied 37mm FLAK 18 anti-aircraft gunfire from the cover of a field of tall crop. China bought an unconfirmed number of these modern guns from Germany in the mid-1930s with some reports stating that sixty were sold to them in 1936.

Chinese Victory at Taierhchuang 24th March - 7th April 1938

A rare modern heavy gun of the Chinese Army is seen here in action at the Battle of Taierhchuang in 1938. It has been set up in a camouflaged in a thatched roofed shelter and fires at distant Japanese targets. The gun is a German FH18 150mm field gun that was supplied to the Chinese in very small numbers in the 1930s. During the Battle at Taierhchuang in Shangtung Province the Chinese defeated the Japanese Imperial Army's 10th Division.

Soldiers of the Chinese 31st Division rush to reinforce the encircling forces that have the Japanese 10th Division trapped in the village of Taierhchuang. The battle which was a costly but welcome victory for the Chiang Kai-shek government resulted in the deaths of about 16,000 Japanese. About 2,000 Japanese did manage to escape from the battle but the victory was welcome news for the Chinese Army even though they suffered about the same casualties as their enemy.

A machine gun team of the 31st Division fire their weapon across the open plain between their position and the besieged Japanese. The troops were part of Li Tsung-jen's 'elite' Kwangsi forces which had a few years earlier been in armed opposition to the Chiang Kai-shek government. In the regional rivalries which plagued China's military capability in the Sino-Japanese War these well trained and well motivated troops were never fully trusted by the Nationalist leader.

Soldiers of the White Sun

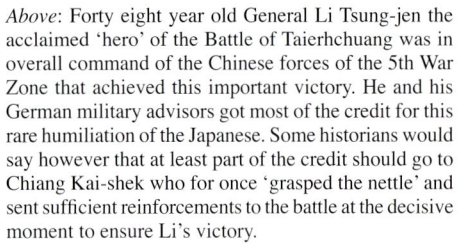

Above: Forty eight year old General Li Tsung-jen the acclaimed 'hero' of the Battle of Taierhchuang was in overall command of the Chinese forces of the 5th War Zone that achieved this important victory. He and his German military advisors got most of the credit for this rare humiliation of the Japanese. Some historians would say however that at least part of the credit should go to Chiang Kai-shek who for once 'grasped the nettle' and sent sufficient reinforcements to the battle at the decisive moment to ensure Li's victory.

Above: A section of infantry move forward at the double during the battle of Taierhchuang as they close the net around the trapped Japanese. These tough and well-equipped soldiers were some of the best in the Chinese Army in 1938 and proved themselves in the bitter fighting. As the Chinese advanced into the Japanese held positions the Imperial Army troops were pushed back against the Grand Canal which ran past the village. The besieged Japanese holding on to a smaller and smaller area were supplied by air drop but most of the food and ammunition fell into Chinese hands.

Right: The Chinese victory over the Japanese at Taierhchuang was headlining news with the majority of people in the west cheering their exploits. This U.S. bubble gum card from 1938 shows the exploits of a small mechanised unit of the Chinese Army which attacked the Japanese across the Grand Canal with amphibious tanks. These cards were quite well researched and mirrored the stories appearing in the U.S. press at the time. According to the caption this victory proved the effectiveness of the 'new' tanks of the Chinese Army over the 'old' Japanese tanks. The Chinese tanks were British made Vickers Cardon Lloyd M1931 light amphibious tanks with a Vickers heavy machine gun as its main armament.

90

China's Continued Resistance, 1938-1941

Above: A resolute and confident looking soldier takes a quick break from the fighting for Taierhchuang behind the shelter of a house wall. He is well prepared for the next advance against Japanese positions with four stick grenades in his canvas carrier. His bandoliers are bulging with plenty of spare clips for his rifle and his bayonet is fixed ready for the signal to attack.

Above: In this patriotic Chinese illustration from 1938 a unit of Nationalist soldiers with bayonets fixed overruns a Japanese position. Propaganda posters had been extremely important to the Nationalists during their rise to power in the late-1920s. During the war against Japan, Chinese artists again produced a large number of patriotic posters. These posters had to get their message across to the largely illiterate Chinese population with images that worked with or without their accompanying slogans.

Above: A well-equipped guerrilla fighter from Shansi Province fires his automatic pistol from a prone position. The C-96 was not a particularly accurate weapon and was would have been not much use in the open terrain he is pictured fighting in. He is at least well dressed in full padded winter uniform with fur lined hood on his jacket and is wearing the type of gas mask often issued to provincial troops.

Right: In what appears to be a 'doctored' photograph two Nationalist women guerrilla fighters pose with their Mauser C-96 'broom-handle' automatic pistols. The girl on the left has her C-96 slung over her shoulder while the older women holds her pistol in readiness. Mauser broom handles would have been a quite suitable weapon for the slightly build Chinese woman. Huge numbers of the German original and various copies were imported during the 1920s and 1930s and many found their way into Guerrilla hands.

91

Soldiers of the White Sun

Another girl fighter poses outside her headquarters wearing a padded coat over the top of her cotton tunic and breeches. This type of double-breasted wadded cotton coat was not issued to most Chinese soldiers who had to make do with padded tunics. She is armed as so many Chinese soldiers were in the 1930s with a Mauser C-96 or one of its many foreign produced copies.

New recruits are put through their paces on the parade ground as the Chinese Army tries to replace some if its losses from the 1937 fighting. The men are wearing newly issued uniforms made out of dark blue or brown cotton cloth with straw sandals. They have all been issued with Hanyang Type 88 rifles and are wearing rather bulky looking ammunition bandoliers. Although the losses suffered by the Nationalist Army in 1937 were heavy, 1938 was to see even worse losses. According to conservative figures issued by the Nationalist government the Army was to lose almost 250,000 dead and almost 486,000 wounded. The parlous state of the Nationalist Army's medical facilities meant that many of the wounded would die later.

These young teenage recruits undergoing target practice in 1938 are replacements for battle losses during the traumatic first year of the war against Japan. They are dressed in a basic cotton uniform worn with straw sandals and have canvas bandoliers which all appear to be empty. Shortage of ammunition would have limited the amount of firing practice that these young soldiers would receive with their 'Chiang Kai-shek' rifles.

In this Nationalist poster of 1938 shows a regular soldier and his guerrilla comrade are shown side by side in their struggle against the Japanese. The caption emphasises this point saying 'The army and the people co-operate to defend South China'.

Enthusiastic young soldiers shout patriotic slogans during a parade in the build up to a Nationalist offensive in 1938. The soldiers are wearing British pattern steel helmets with their light khaki cotton uniforms. They are armed with Mauser rifles while the machine gunner in the foreground has the Czechoslovakian ZB-26 light machine gun. He wears leather pouches around his waist which carry spare magazines and an oiling and cleaning kit.

A bodyguard unit of a Chinese commander go through arms drill on the parade ground in the summer of 1938. This 'elite' unit are unusually wearing stiff cork pith helmets with the Nationalist sun emblem on the front. Several types of cork sun helmet were worn by the Nationalist Army during the period and this model is similar in shape to those worn by Western polo players. The men have woollen dark khaki tunics and trousers and puttees with leather boots and have full equipment. Equipment includes backpacks and brown leather accoutrements for their Mauser C-96 broom handle pistols.

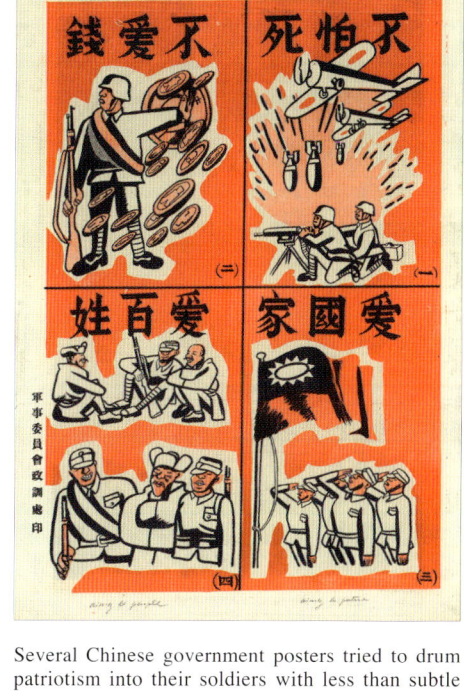

Several Chinese government posters tried to drum patriotism into their soldiers with less than subtle messages. This storyboard poster from 1938 says, 'Don't fear death, don't love money, love the nation, love the people'.

Two machine gunners blast their Browning heavy machine gun at the Japanese from the protection of their trench. The firer is exposing himself to enemy fire by crouching on the platform built to stand his machine gun on while the loader shelters in the trench. Both men have improvised backpacks on with canvas strapping holding their blanket rolls and spare pair of shoes in place.

In a photograph taken from a Chinese propaganda magazine of the period an officer of the 21st Divisional Artillery uses a rangefinder on the Yangtze Front. Although his rank bar on his collar is not clear in this photograph it appears that he is a Captain. There are three three-pointed stars on a coloured background in the colour of the wearer's branch which in the case of the Artillery was blue.

Soldiers of the White Sun

Soldiers leave for the front on an overloaded troop train from Shansi Province in 1938 and their defiant cheers are echoed by the locals who have gathered to see them off. The men look well motivated and are well kitted out for the fighting with M35 steel helmets and padded winter uniforms. Two of the men have the leather pouches to carry spare magazines for their light machine guns while another three have brown leather equipment for the broom handle pistol. The unit standard bearer carries the flag furled with a canvas cover over it to protect it during the journey.

Smartly dressed officers inspect their men on the parade ground in front of their regimental standard in 1938. Nationalist military flags followed the same basic pattern with a blue field with a red square panel in the centre. The white sun emblem was originally the symbol of the Kuomintang Party of Sun Yat-sen and was adopted as the national symbol in 1928. Unit parade flags had as in this case a white panel running down the hoist with black characters which described the name of the unit. If a parade flag was representing a particular unit it usually had a yellow fringe around the edge. When the flag was used to represent the whole Nationalist Army it had no fringe and no white panel. The army flag was never however flown from a flagpole on parade as the national flag was always used. As in the U.S. Army, smaller guidon flags were carried at times and had the same design as the larger version.

In what appears to be an action photograph a concealed German 20mm Flak 30 fires at Japanese aircraft flying overhead. Even major Chinese cities were defended by only a handful of anti-aircraft guns with for instance Canton having only three batteries of 75mm guns and twenty lighter guns like the 20mm's seen here.

Right: This page from a 1938 Japanese children's book on the war in China is typical of the brightly coloured pictures in these widely distributed propaganda books. It shows the 'cowardly' Chinese soldiers panicking before the onslaught of the heroic Japanese Army. Racist imagery like this was designed to convince the Japanese public no matter how young that the Chinese people were sub-human and could be treated as inhumanely as necessary. Other illustrations in books aimed at the same age group show and describe the Chinese Army arms and equipment in detail, as if preparing the young reader for the day when they might also fight against them.

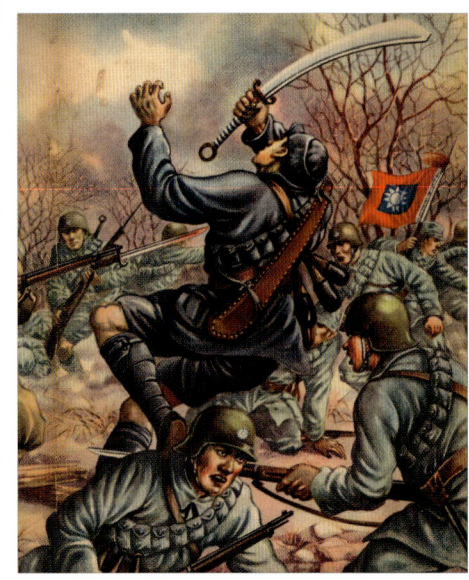

China's Continued Resistance, 1938-1941

Above: This heavily camouflaged Flak 30 and its equally well-hidden crew is firing from the hills surrounding a Chinese city in 1938. Lighter calibre guns like this 20mm were deployed to protect railway junctions and other strategic points and were easily moved from one site to another. Because of the shortage of heavier weaponry every effort was made to remove artillery and other equipment before a city or strategic point fell to the Japanese. After the fall of the Nationalist capital Nanking in December 1937 the larger anti-aircraft guns were concentrated in Canton. When that city in turn fell most of the remaining artillery were used to defend the new capital, Chungking.

Top right: A crewman of a Flak 30 anti-aircraft gun uses a hand held rangefinder to direct the fire of his comrades. The rangefinder is supported by a metal bracket which is worn on the soldiers shoulder to take the weight of the device and to keep it steady. He along with the rest of the crew has fastened foliage to his back in an effort to camouflage himself and the gun from ground attack.

Right: A propaganda photo montage from a Chinese news magazine of 1938 shows a soldier standing symbolic guard over the nationalities that made up China. The soldier himself represents the majority Chinese while the four civilians represent the minority Manchu, Mongol, Tibetan and Moslem sections of the 400 million population. Symbolism like this was intended to unite the minority peoples of China behind the struggle against the Japanese invader.

Soldiers of the White Sun

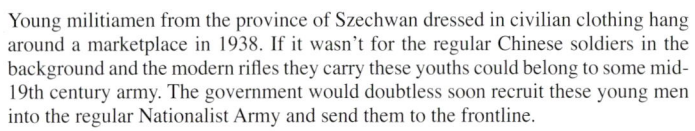

Young militiamen from the province of Szechwan dressed in civilian clothing hang around a marketplace in 1938. If it wasn't for the regular Chinese soldiers in the background and the modern rifles they carry these youths could belong to some mid-19th century army. The government would doubtless soon recruit these young men into the regular Nationalist Army and send them to the frontline.

In this bubble gun card published in the U.S. in 1938 Chiang Kai-shek is shown rather fancifully commanding his troops in the field. The caption to the card describes the scene as, "Generalissimo Chiang Kai-shek personally commands his troops at Chengchow at the Western end of the Yellow River Front". These cards fed the U.S. public's interest in the war in China which was featured heavily in the 240 card series along with the Spanish Civil War.

Chiang Kai-shek's face was seen on the cover of many worldwide magazines as the crisis between China and Japan erupted into full-scale war in the summer of 1937. This photograph is on the cover of one of the many war pictorial magazines published in China at the time. The caption to the photograph reads, "General Chiang Kai-shek, the highest Anti-Japanese Commander that deserves the esteem and support of the whole of China".

This section of a larger illustration from 1938 shows the mobilisation of the Chinese people against the Japanese invader. During the first few years of the Sino-Japanese War the Chinese people were largely behind the Nationalist government. However the patriotism shown in propaganda pictures like this was hard to maintain after years of defeats at the hands of the Japanese.

China's Continued Resistance, 1938-1941

A soldier of the Chinese Army studies the characters carved into the butt of a Japanese Arisaka rifle captured at the Battle of Chuen-Yang on the 20th of December 1938. During the first year of the Sino-Japanese War, Chinese successes were few and far between and always short lived. The soldier is unusually well equipped and has the winter hat worn by some Northern Chinese troops at the start of the war as well as a rare backpack.

Relaxed sentries guard an airfield and smile for the camera while having a smoke break from their duties in 1939. Their jackets demonstrate the variation in shade of the Nationalist Army's khaki summer uniform. Cotton shorts worn with puttees and sandals are typical of the soldiers of Southern China who were lucky to receive any kind of winter uniform. They are well armed with Mauser rifles and have the basic equipment of canvas bandoliers with one slung over the shoulder and one tied around the waist.

An Anti-aircraft crewmen parade with their German supplied light anti-aircraft guns wearing French Adrian style helmets. This photograph was taken in the province of Yunnan near to the border with French Indo-China. French arms and equipment could before the takeover of the colony by the Japanese in 1941 be easily shipped across the border into Southwest China.

Right: This cover of the Eastern Pictorial magazine of October 1939 features a smiling General Wei Li-huang one of the more able Nationalist officers. General Wei, born in 1897 was at that time the Commander of the 1st War Area as well as commanding the 14th Army Group. He went on to serve with some success as Commander in Chief of the Chinese Yunnan Expeditionary Force from 1942-1944. In the 1946-1949 Civil War he was in command of all the Nationalist forces in Manchuria during the ill-fated campaign against the Communists.

Soldiers of the White Sun

The four photographs on this page show female volunteers preparing to defend Chungking in 1941. In the first photo we can see teenage girls drilling at their barracks armed with Mauser rifles, while the second shows a smiling sentry on the hills above the Nationalist wartime capital. Uniforms consist of simple cotton dresses with the volunteers name and unit on the cloth patch above the left breast in the same fashion as their male comrades wear on their tunics. The next two photographs show the same type of volunteers marching and combat training with full equipment and wearing large sun hats. Foliage has been fixed to the hats for camouflage and they are armed with Mauser Karabiner 98a carbines.

China's Continued Resistance, 1938-1941

The crew of a German manufactured searchlight go through anti-aircraft drill on the outskirts of Chungking in 1941. They also had a few sound detectors that had been imported from Germany during the 1930s. This equipment had been evacuated from one of the cities captured by the Japanese in 1937-1938. When the Chinese capital was moved to Chungking in October 1938 all available anti-aircraft guns were moved to defend the city.

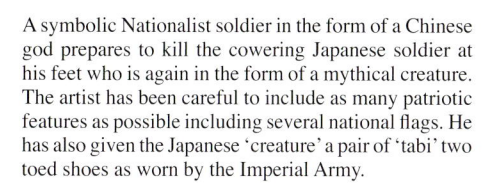

A symbolic Nationalist soldier in the form of a Chinese god prepares to kill the cowering Japanese soldier at his feet who is again in the form of a mythical creature. The artist has been careful to include as many patriotic features as possible including several national flags. He has also given the Japanese 'creature' a pair of 'tabi' two toed shoes as worn by the Imperial Army.

These two photographs show the men crewing rangefinders for the light anti-aircraft batteries defending Chungking in 1941. The capital was given warning of Japanese air attack by a series of twenty-two alarm stations around the city. However with only a few batteries of 75mm guns available to defend Chungking the city was more or less helpless. Known at the time as the most bombed place on earth at the time between 1939 and 1941 it suffered 142 raids.

Soldiers of the White Sun

Below: A motorcycle and sidecar of a 'special' Chinese unit formed to combat the enemy's possible use of parachutists demonstrate their signalling skills in January 1941. It was always possible for the Chinese to equip small elite units like this that could be parading in front of the press. The driver is armed with a Mauser Kar.98k rifle white the signaller has a C-96 broom handle automatic pistol.

A nice close up of a motorcycle and sidecar combination crew shows the driver with a pillion passenger behind and their comrade sat in the sidecar. All three men wear the German M35 helmet with the Nationalist sun badge on the left side and have a formation patch loosely sewn on their left sleeves. The driver seems to be the only one with a pair of goggles and the rest of their equipment is pretty basic with canvas bandoliers to carry clips for their 'Chiang Kai-shek' Mauser Kar.98k rifles.

This cover from The Standard Photo News of the 24th of January 1942 has two motorcyclists and sidecar crews from the anti-parachutist unit. The unit is equipped with Zundapp motorcycles and sidecars left over from the German arms shipments of the late-1930s. German Army versions would have a light machine gun mounted in the sidecar but this crew is armed only with their Mauser type 'Chiang Kai-shek' rifles.

This rapid response motorised unit is part of the defence forces of the Nationalist capital of Chungking in January 1941. The unit made up of handful of German supplied Sfz. scout cars and motorcycles was intended to counter any Japanese parachutists who might attack the city. Germany's use of paratroopers during the Blitzkrieg campaigns of 1940 had made the Chinese paranoid about Japan's possible use of similar tactics. According to the original caption for the photograph the Japanese were reported to be training special attack units in occupied China.

China's Continued Resistance, 1938-1941

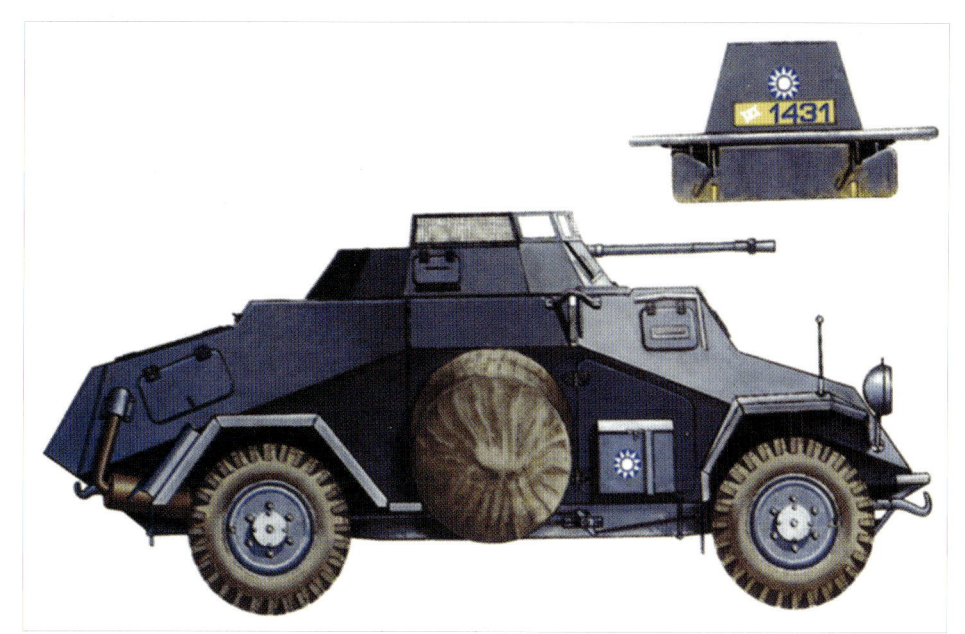

This profile of a Sfz.222 scout car shows the colour scheme that they were delivered in and the markings carried by them. As far as is known the scout cars were not given any camouflage paint and were used in their grey delivery colour. The Nationalist sun emblem was carried on the side and at the front of the vehicle with the vehicle number.

The crew of this German made Sfz.222 scout car bring the armoured vehicles armament of a 20mm KWK 30 cannon and MG Model 13 machine gun into action. These lightly armoured scout cars along with a few Panzer I light tanks were supplied to China between 1936-1938. After 1938 the changing world situation meant that no further arms could be expected to be exported from Germany for use against their new ally Japan.

Throughout the Sino-Japanese War the advances of the Japanese Army left groups of Chinese regular soldiers cut off from the central government. This group of Nationalist soldiers have retreated inland from the Japanese occupation of the Chinese coastline. They look like a mixture of regular and guerrilla fighters with only a few having steel helmets and any semblance of uniform. Men like this had three choices, either to become guerrillas and fight behind Japanese lines usually without government support. Alternatively they could join the Communists as many chose to either through necessity or political conviction. Or they could try and join the puppet armies which were recruited by the Wang Ching-wei government after 1940. Whole units of Nationalist troops went over to the Japanese controlled government in Nanking, not through any liking for Wang Ching-wei but simply to survive. The Nanking 'puppet' Army reached a strength of several hundred thousand men by 1945 usually through recruiting ex-Nationalist troops.

Right: General Hsueh Yueh 'Little Tiger' was the victorious commander of the Chinese forces which won the 3rd Battle of Changhsha in late-1941/early-1942. Hsueh Yueh who was in charge of the 9th War Area decisively defeated the Japanese Imperial Army's 11th Army. His tactic was to allow the Japanese to advance to the outskirts of Changsha in Hunan Province before enveloping them with superior Chinese forces. The Japanese retreated from the battlefield having suffered a rare defeat and having lost a considerable number of men.

101

Soldiers of the White Sun

Above: Nationalist troops manhandle an early wooden wheeled version of the PAK 35/36 37mm anti-tank gun into position overlooking the Yangtze River in November 1941. The gun was according to the caption to be used to harass Japanese launches running supplies up and down the river. China imported 100 of this early version of the German anti-tank gun as well as at least twenty-four of the rubber tire version

Below: A German made PAK 35/36 anti-tank gun crew move their gun into position in the undergrowth in Kiangsi province before a Japanese attack in 1941. As with all the German supplied heavy weaponry these modern anti-tank guns were supplied to Chiang Kai-shek's most favoured German trained Divisions. Most of these divisions along with nearly all of their equipment had been lost in the fighting of 1937-1938.

China's Continued Resistance, 1938-1941

A formation of well turned out infantry line up outside their barracks in 1941 for an inspection wearing uniforms in varying shades of summer khaki. The khaki tunics, shorts and puttees vary from a very light sandy shade to a medium brown or green colour. All of the rank and file have rice tubes over their left shoulders which would also hold personal items. While the two main groups of men in the foreground all wear the field cap again in varying shades of khaki the men stood against the wall in the background are wearing steel helmets.

On the 12th of May 1941 an assault party crosses the Yellow River to its north bank ready to attack the Japanese in the Chung-tiao Shan region. The men under their officer's instructions nervously train their 'Hanyang' rifles on the enemy held opposite bank. At the same time they are trying to find what little cover their wooden river junk which is serving as an improvised assault boat will give them. Backpacks worn by the men are in several types and have been made by the men themselves using a bamboo frame and army issue blankets.

Chinese machine gunners captured by the Japanese are made to pose with their weapons over their shoulders for the news cameras. The future for Chinese soldiers captured by the Japanese Imperial Army was bleak with most being quickly executed. This was especially the case in the first years of the Sino-Japanese War, but as the war wound into the early-1940s some were given another option. With the establishment of the 'puppet' government of Wang Ching-wei in Nanking in 1940 defeated units were offered the chance to join its army. When the only other alternative was death it is understandable that some Nationalist soldiers chose to join the 'quisling' Nanking Army.

The Chinese Army in Burma 1942

The Japanese invasion of Burma in December 1941 and their likely defeat of the British forces defending the country threatened China's vital supply lines along the Burma Road. Chiang Kai-shek agreed reluctantly to send Chinese troops into northern Burma to help the British hold a defensive line. In January 1942 a Chinese Expeditionary Force made up of nine under strength divisions crossed the border. Included in the Chinese force was the 200th Division which had the only substantial tank force in the whole of the army. During the course of the Burma Campaign the Chinese formations performance was mixed with the 200th, 22nd and 38th Divisions putting up a good performance. The 200th Division held the Japanese for twelve days at Toungoo while the 38th pushed back a strong Japanese force surrounding British troops at Yenangyaung, allowing them to withdraw. After the Japanese pushed the British back into retreat the surviving Chinese troops either withdrew back into China or in the case of the 22nd and 38th into India where they were to be re-trained and equipped by the Allies.

During the fighting at Pyu south of Toungoo in Burma in March 1942 this Chinese infantryman heavily camouflaged with foliage rushes forward at the double to the attack. He carries his Mauser rifle slung from his shoulder and tucked under his arm with bayonet fixed in readiness. This soldier belongs to the Chinese force which had marched 800 miles from Yunnan Province to support the British withdrawal from Burma.

This line of Soviet supplied T-26B light tanks belong to the 200th Mechanised Division which was the only large armoured formation in the Chinese Army before 1942. The 200th Brigade with its eighty T-26Bs was to fight in the Burmese Campaign of 1942 where it performed well. When the surrounded Division was ordered to retreat back to China it had to abandon all the precious T-26s. The surviving crews then had to make their way in small groups back through the jungle to Chinese lines.

The Chinese Army in Burma, 1942

Above: This Soviet supplied T-26 Model 1933 light tank is one of eighty-seven which were delivered to the Chinese in 1938. Most of the T-26's went to make up the 200th Mechanised Division which lost its equipment in Burma. Also supplied by the Soviet Union were small numbers of FAI and BA-6 armoured cars as well as a few T-27 tankettes. These other types appear to have been kept well away from the fighting as there is no photographic evidence of their use in combat.

Above: Soldiers of the Chinese Expeditionary Force in Burma barter with locals for food during their campaign in the northeast of the country. Altogether nine Chinese Divisions were involved in attempts to relieve the British position until May 1942. Divisions in the Chinese Army were generally smaller than in the Allied Armies with a typical one being equivalent to a Brigade in the British Army. The poor behaviour of some Chinese troops during their retreat through Burma led to resentment from the locals. Burmese bandits or 'dacoits' also took advantage of the Chinese soldiers plight and attacked them in turn.

Right: On the 15th of April 1942, General Sun Li-jen the commanding officer of the Chinese 38th Division in Burma discusses joint operations with Lieutenant-General T.J. Hutton and other British officers. General Hutton was General Officer commanding 'Burma Command' from late-December 1941 until March 1942. General Sun Li-jen as one of the most capable Nationalist Army commanders during the war went on to command larger formations throughout the Burma Campaign.

Above: Soldiers of the 38th Division fraternise with the crew of a Stuart M3 light tank of the British 7th Armoured Brigade at Yenangyaung in Central Burma. The British tanks had supported the Chinese troops during their relief of the British 1st Burma Division which was surrounded by the advancing Japanese 33rd Division. Although stationed to protect the Yenangyaung Oilfields in the background both the British and Chinese had to soon retreat northwards towards the safety of the Indian border.

Right: Lieutenant-General Joseph.W. Stilwell (1883-1946) known as 'Vinegar Joe' was at first glance an obvious choice to be the USA's senior military representative in China. Stilwell had served in China as U.S. Military Attache from 1935 to 1939 and had also learned to speak Chinese during the 1920s. He arrived in China in March 1942 and was sent immediately to Burma to try and help the withdrawal of the Chinese Expeditionary Force fighting there. Stilwell was instrumental in the plan to retrain large numbers of Chinese troops in Allied training camps. His relationship with Chiang Kai-shek was however strained and his poor opinion of his Allied counterparts led to problems. After failing in his attempts to be put in command of the whole of the Chinese Army he was recalled to the USA in late 1944. Although a good soldier, Stilwell was a poor diplomat and lacked the subtlety needed to deal with the Chinese leadership.

105

China at War, 1942-1943

The stalemate which existed in China during 1942 and 1943 was largely a result of Japan's concentration on its Pacific Campaign. Fighting in mainland China did continue but on a much reduced scale with the Japanese Imperial Army not planning to extend their area of occupation. Most Japanese operations were really nothing but large scale raids to subdue the population where necessary and gather rice and other crops. Campaigns in May-September 1942 in the Chekiang-Kiangsi region and Western Hupeh in May-June 1943 did involve large numbers of troops. The campaign in Chekiang-Kiangsi involved elements of forty-two Chinese divisions facing seven Japanese divisions and several Independent Brigades. Fighting in Western Hupeh in May-June 1943 involved four Japanese divisions as well as units from a further two divisions. They were facing divisions from the 6th War Area made up of four army groups with forty-one divisions. Even though the Chinese order of battle for these campaigns show a vast 'on paper' superiority over their Japanese foe this is misleading. Chinese units were nearly always greatly under strength and poorly equipped and were usually committed to battle 'piece meal'. This meant that any superiority of the Chinese Nationalist Army over the Japanese Imperial Army was purely notional. Chinese battlefield casualties during 1942-1943 reduced over the 1937-1938 period but were still high with 247,000 in 1942, and 163,000 in 1943.

Chiang Kai-shek rides his white charger during a military review at an officers training academy. Chiang began his military career as did many Chinese officers at the time at a Japanese military academy. From 1911 he fought on the side of the revolutionaries in China before joining Sun Yat-sen at Canton. He had been continuously at war since 1924 first against the Warlords, then against the Japanese and Communists. His failure to unite China full behind him was to lead to the Civil War from 1946 and his defeat by the Communists in 1949.

In a wartime speech Chiang Kai-shek exhorts his men to continue the fight against the Japanese invaders. Chiang's stubborn insistence on China's continued resistance against the Japanese meant that they had to commit over one-million men to the theatre. It would have been far easier for Chiang to come to an accommodation with the Japanese and to have even formed a military alliance with them against the Communists. His hatred of the Communists could well have pushed him into making peace with the Japanese but their bestial treatment of the Chinese population made this impossible.

The larger than life 'Christian Warlord' General Feng Yu-hsiang writes a letter at his desk in Chungking in 1942. General Feng had been one of the most powerful figures in Chinese politics during the 1920s when he controlled large and well-trained armies. He brought his Kuomichun 'Peoples Army' into the Nationalist camp during their Northern Expedition of 1926-1928 but he was never a firm supporter of Chiang Kai-shek. He revolted against the Nationalist government in 1929 and was defeated and went into exile. He was eventually allowed to return to a role in the Chinese Army and served on the national military council from 1935. Chiang kai-shek made sure that any post that he held did not put him into a position where he could again be a threat to the central government.

On the Yellow River Front under the shade of trees in a public park a group of officer trainees receive instruction. They are being taught about the finer points of a Chinese made Type 24 heavy machine gun when used in the anti-aircraft role. The Type 24 was a copy of the German Maxim M1908 and was the main heavy machine gun of the Chinese Army until the end of the Civil War in 1949. All Chinese Group Armies by the mid-1940s had Officer Training Corps which gave refresher training to officers who were not in the frontline.

Right: Two Chinese soldiers demonstrate clearly their use of captured Japanese weapons and equipment by firing a couple of Type 89 50mm 'knee mortars' while wearing M32 helmets. During the fighting during the Salween Campaign some Chinese soldiers were killed by their own side when wearing Japanese helmets and items of uniforms. This was because they were so short of helmets that they took any captured ones and wore them without wearing a distinguishing field signs. The Type 89 was basically a grenade projector that if fired from the knee as its nickname might suggest would badly fracture the firer's leg. According to stories of the time a number of Allied troops did try firing the mortar from the knee before word got around about the stupidity of this practice.

Soldiers of the White Sun

A cavalry unit advances through flooded terrain in the early-1940s would have to keep on the look out for Japanese aircraft. The Chinese cavalry in the main fronts were by this period were really mounted infantry and the shortage of horses meant that it was difficult to raise new units.

A U.S. issued poster stamp from 1942 commemorates the five years of China's struggle against the Japanese invaders. With words like 'Fight the War and Build the Country' it suggests that the U.S. would support Chiang Kai-shek in the long term. Symbolism is important with the Chinese dragon slaying the 'evil' Japanese octopus whose tentacles had reached out over much of Asia by 1942.

This M24 heavy machine gunner photographed in 1942 is wearing a typical cotton summer uniform. On the left sleeve of his jacket he has a unit patch and he also has a Nationalist sun cloth badge on the front of his basketwork sun hat. Underneath the sun hat he is wearing a ski type cap made from the same rough cotton as his jacket. The reverse swastika symbol on the breechblock of his machine gun was used as a good luck symbol in China as well as in many other parts of the orient.

A British poster of the early-1940s featuring a Chinese civilian emphasises the fact that China's war against Japan is now part of the greater World War. It calls for contributions to the China Aid Fund to help with humanitarian schemes in un-occupied China.

Above: Soldiers take a relaxation break relatively safe from Japanese air attack in a hillside cave in 1942. The Chinese soldier had little in the way of R&R and these men look to have been given pamphlets with selected speeches of Chiang Kai-shek to read. Boredom and hunger often led to soldiers preying on the livestock and crops of the local population that they were supposed to be protecting. This was particularly the case when stationed away from their own province in an area whose population they felt no real affinity with. Although looking relaxed the men have their ZB-26 light machine gun and Mauser Kar.98k rifles to hand in case of enemy attack.

Right: Two eighteen year old recruits train with a ZB-26 light machine gun in November 1942 having been conscripted four months before. These young soldiers are typical of the millions that were sacrificed during the war against Japan. The ZB-26 was the standard light machine gun of the Chinese Army during the latter-1930s and throughout the 1940s.

Soldiers of the White Sun

Central Military Academies, 1942-1945

Cadets from the Chengtu Military Academy perform a march past on the parade ground of their training facility in 1942 wearing German M35 steel helmets. Their status as cadets is indicated by the circular plastic discs on their collars and although not visible they also probably have arm badges on their left sleeves. Better trained units like this one were however the exception not the rule in the Chinese Army in the early-1940s. The men are well kitted out and have a high level of equipment with backpacks as well as leather belts and pouches. They are mostly armed with Mauser rifles but the man in the centre has a Belgian made FN Mle-30 heavy automatic rifle.

Opposite
Top: Cadets undergo drill on the parade ground of the Chengtu Military Academy and hold their Hanyang Type 88 rifles over their heads. These young officer cadets would soon be sent to the frontline and given immediate command as junior officers. In order to fill the huge gaps in the officer ranks left by five years of war with Japan new academies had to be established. Under the old pre-1937 system too few cadets had graduated from the Central Military Academy. Between 1929 and 1937 the Central Military Academy had only turned out 3,000 new officers per year. Just to replace losses of junior officers in the existing Chinese divisions this had to be expanded three times over. To order to form any new divisions the figure had to be expanded by at the very least four times.

Bottom: Trainees from the 19th Regiment of the Nationalist Army at the 'S' branch of the Central Military Academy march past at a speed called 'bent-knee goose step', other speeds used by the parade ground training officer are 'dogtrot' and 'route march'. The men aim to impress the reviewing officers by carrying their heavy Type 24 heavy machine guns on their shoulders. The cosmopolitan nature of the Chinese Army's arms supplies is shown by the Soviet Moisin-Nagant M1891 rifles with fixed bayonets carried by the men at the back of the column.

At the same parade at Chengtu Military Academy the training regiment's flag is paraded past the reviewing stand by these well turned out cadets. The flag bearer must be an officer as he has high leather boots while his men have puttees and leather shoes. All Nationalist unit flags had a red field with a blue rectangle in the centre with a white KMT sun on it. If the flag was ceremonial it would have a yellow fringe around it as in this case and would vary in size depending on the unit it represented.

China at War, 1942-1943

Soldiers of the White Sun

Left: Smartly turned out troops at one of the national training centres march past the reviewing stand in good order. They all wear the German supplied M35 steel helmet which was still in use with some units until the end of the Civil War in 1949. According to some sources there were only about 300,000 of this model helmet imported by China during the 1930s. Other more realistic sources state that the true number was several million and certainly this seems a more believable figure bearing in mind the frequency that they were seen between 1937-1949.

越接近勝利
越要堅苦奮鬥
軍委會政治部製

Above: This poster from 1942 shows a defiant Chinese soldier standing in defence of the Nationalist sun. Its caption reads, "The Closer We Are to Victory, the Harder We Must Struggle".

Left: Trainees at the Pihu training centre in Szechwan Province undergo gas drill as part of their training course in 1943. Unlike the conflict in Europe, the threat of gas attack by the Japanese was very real as the Imperial Army employed chemical weapons on a number of occasions. During the Battle of Yichang in October 1941 for instance the Japanese fired 1,000 mustard 'yellow' gas shells and 1,500 so-called 'red' gas shells. The red gas was a sneeze and nausea chemical which was intended to incapacitate the victim during an attack.

China at War, 1942-1943

A squad of trainee 'commandos' undergo training under the watchful eyes of a visiting British military delegation at Pihu training centre in 1943. The young soldiers are all dressed in rough cotton uniforms and are well equipped with haversacks, canvas holdalls and bandoliers for their Mauser rifles.

Soldiers climb aboard junks to take them up river on the Yangtze Front on the 19th of July 1943. In an attempt to make up the shortage of helmets these men have mostly been issued with basketwork hats. These hats look in shape like a cross between a pith helmet and a German steel helmet and carry the Nationalist sun emblem in the same place as the M35. Chinese soldiers were rarely seen bareheaded and the imitation headgear is better than nothing and could at least provide a little shelter from the rain.

Sergeant T Chi-Yuan, a hero of the Chinese Army on the Yangtze Front pictured here in July 1943 was reported to have personally killed 100 Japanese! The photograph captions states that the Sergeant killed all these Japanese during the Upper Yangtze Battle of late May early June. His uniform is a simple light khaki cotton shirt and shorts with a raffia type pith helmet with a Nationalist badge added to the front.

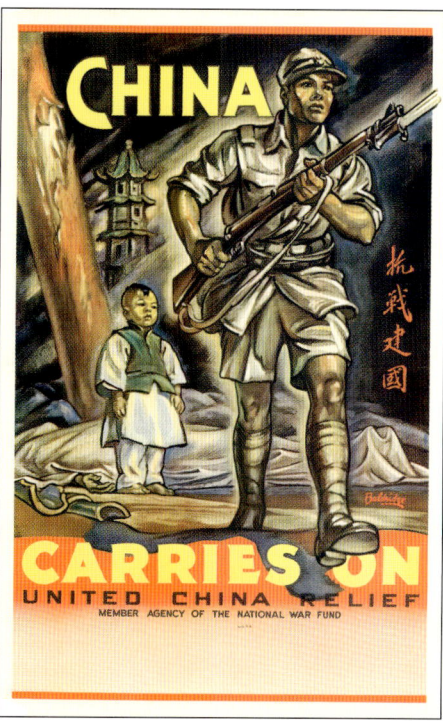

Several posters were issued by the United China Relief Fund during the 1942-1945 period and this example emphasises that China was still fighting. The brave Chinese soldier defends the helpless children of his nation symbolised by the boy with his dead mother at his feet.

Soldiers of the White Sun

Chiang Kai-shek and his Deputy Chief of Staff, General Pai Hsung-hsi stood on his left shoulder inspect a line up of high ranking officers in Chungking in 1943. Born in 1893, General Pai Hsung-hsi graduated from the Paoting Military Academy in 1916 and fought during the Nationalist's Northern Expedition of 1926-1927. He was one of the most reliable of Chiang Kai-shek's generals serving in several capacities as heads of military councils and committees.

Generalissimo Chiang Kai-shek reviews some of his men outside their barracks in 1943. The Nationalist Chinese government had many weaknesses and was under foreign attack for most of its existence and it was largely the force of Chiang Kai-shek's personality that held it together. Chiang wears his usual officers service uniform with the addition of a pair of white parade gloves and rides a black horse instead of his famous white stallion. General Chang Chi-Chung is riding behind the Generalissimo and his mount does not seem to be a particularly fine specimen of horseflesh.

A column of enthusiastic soldiers pictured in 1943 sing patriotic songs as they march to battle wearing typical winter uniforms. The padded jackets are in various shades of blue-grey as are the winter version of the standard cotton ski cap. Winter hats when issued, would be made of quilted cotton with earflaps lined which warmer material. Trousers worn by these troops again vary in shade and are held at the knees with woollen or other cloth puttees. Rifles carried by these men are a mixture of Hanyang Type 88s and more modern Mauser's imported during the 1930s from various countries.

In this photograph dated June 1943 Chinese casualties are being carried by stretcher parties back from the fighting on the Yunnan Front. The chances of survival for a wounded Chinese soldier were pretty slim with much of the medical care being given to them being rudimentary. However the biggest killer amongst the Chinese soldier was not being killed or wounded in battle but disease. For every Chinese soldier who died of a wound, ten were dying of dysentery or malaria or other tropical diseases. The poor general health of the average Chinese recruit did not help and many even died on their way from recruitment centres to the training camps.

Firing from behind a village wall these soldiers fighting in the summer of 1943 are armed with the usual mix of weaponry. The machine gun is the Finnish M26 while the small grenade launcher appears to be a locally made version of the Japanese knee mortar.

A machine gun crew emerge from their underground shelter into the trench system surrounding the city of Tungkwan in the Summer of 1943. These men belong to a 300,000 strong army under the command of General Hu Tsung-nan who is in charge of the 1st War Area. They are armed with the Finnish made Lahti Saloranti M26 light machine gun which was only exported to China and their rifles are Czech VZ-24s.

Soldiers of the White Sun

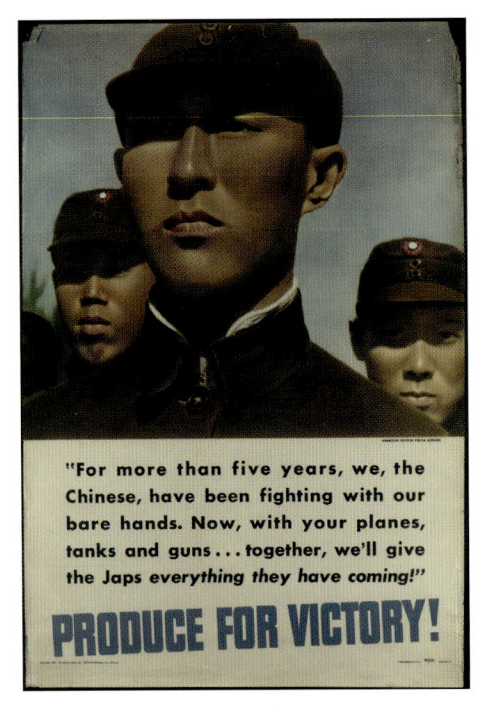

"For more than five years, we, the Chinese, have been fighting with our bare hands. Now, with your planes, tanks and guns... together, we'll give the Japs everything they have coming!"

PRODUCE FOR VICTORY!

Above: A British ministry of war poster from 1942 urges all efforts to be made to produce more armaments to supply the Chinese who have been fighting the Japanese for five years. The Chinese were never happy with the amount of material support they received from the Allies. They perceived not without some justification that far more military aid was going to other allied nations. For instance the Free French received slightly over double the amount of lend lease support that they did!

Right
Top: This cavalry flag bearer and his unit are on parade in Shansi Province in the summer of 1943. The unit displayed their prowess as horsemen to the visiting Western Press who were often shown troops in the safer far flung regions of Free China.

Bottom: These very smartly turned out cavalry troopers from the Shansi in 1943 are well mounted on their Mongolian ponies. Although cavalry were of little use in the main theatres of war in 1937-1945 they still had a important role in the wide open spaces of North West China.

Battle of Changteh, 1943

Left: Infantry advance into the much fought over city of Changteh in China's rice bowl on the 9th of December 1943. The city changed hands four times in forty days and less than twenty-four of its 10,000 buildings were reported to be undamaged by the end of the fighting. According to the original caption to the photograph only 300 of the Nationalist 57th Division which fought for the city survived the battle. During the closely fought battle three Divisional commanders of the Nationalist Army were killed in action.

Below: After the final victory over the Japanese in the Battle of Changteh in December 1943 the commanding officer of the 57th Division, General Yu Cheng-wan (third from left) poses with some of his staff. Behind the General is the Central Bank of Changteh County which served as his headquarters during the battle.

Soldiers of the White Sun

Above: Soldiers bring in two surrendered Japanese soldiers to their headquarters during the Battle of Changteh. The dejected and ashamed Japanese soldiers were paraded in front of the press as their Chinese captors made the most of their victory.

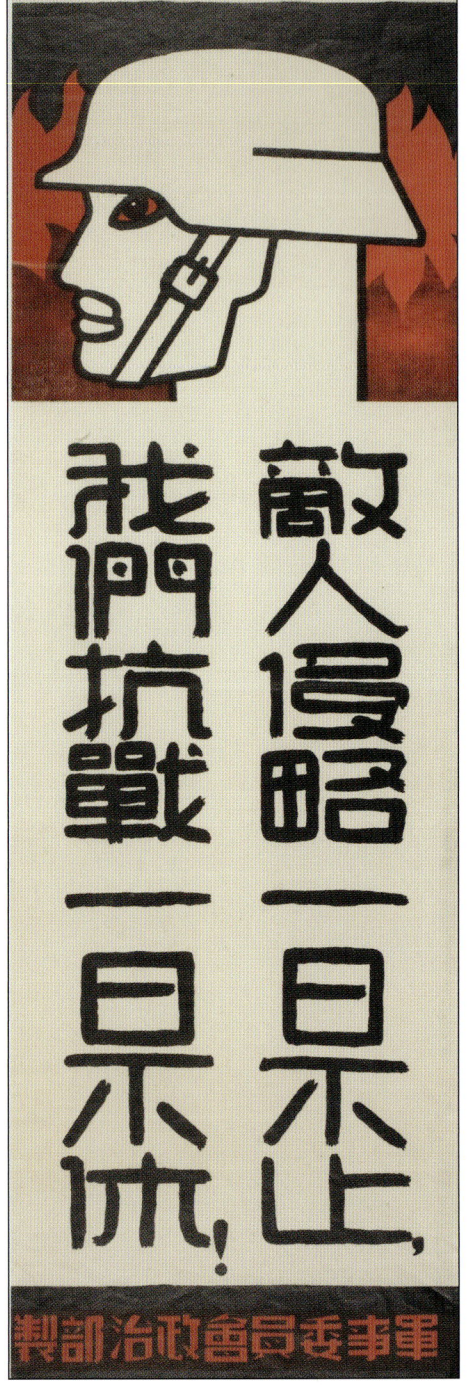

Above: This 1942 poster carries the slogan, "The longer we fight, the stronger we become. The longer our enemy fights, the weaker he becomes." The stylised image of the Chinese soldier wearing the German pattern helmet has the flames of war behind it.

Left: This rare sight of a surrendered Japanese soldier was captured for the world press and was captioned "Son of the Rising Sun in defeat". He was one of a handful of Japanese soldiers captured during the Chinese victory at Changteh in December 1943. This early in the Second World War it was almost unknown for a Japanese Imperial soldiers to allow themselves to fall into enemy hands. His shame is evident in his face while his captors seem to be looking at him with a mixture of hatred and curiosity.

U.S., Soviet and British military officers examine captured Japanese weapons and equipment captured by the Chinese after Japans defeat at Changteh. Chinese officers proudly show off their spoils to their Allies which include M32 helmets and officers swords.

Sentries guard a cache of captured Japanese small arms taken during the Battle of Changteh. All of the five machine guns stacked on the ground are Taisho-11s which would be turned against their former owners if enough ammunition is available. The soldier on the left of the photograph is armed with a MP-28 and has spare magazines in the two leather pouches he wears on his chest.

A long column of infantry march through the ruins of Changteh with their officer riding at their head. Changteh had great strategic significance and was at the heart of China's rice growing area. Before withdrawing from the city the Japanese had destroyed all the rice stores they could to stop the Chinese getting hold of them.

Major-General Ou Chen, the commander of the 4th Corps of the 9th War Area and was one of the heroes of the Battle of Changteh in November-December 1943. During the bitter fighting for the strategically important city the Chinese suffered heavy casualties before making a fighting retreat. A few days after their withdrawal large Chinese reinforcements counterattacked and drove the Japanese from the city.

Allied Training Centres: Ramgarh and Yunnan, 1942-1943

The Chinese troops of the 22nd and 38th Division that had retreated from the Burmese campaign in 1942 were eventually evacuated to India. These troops were to be trained under Allied instructors and were to be armed and equipped by the USA to help in the eventual retaking of Burma. A large-scale training centre was set up in a former British facility in Behar which had previously been used as a POW camp. Money was provided by the British while the U.S. Army provided instructors to re-train Chinese troops in most aspects of modern warfare. Courses were taught in artillery, small arms, signals, radios and the care of draught animals which would be needed in the Burmese terrain. Other troops were flown over the Himalayas from China with the best recruits being taken onto the Ramgarh training courses. These newly trained troops were formed into the New 1st Army under the command of General Sun Li-jen and the New 6th Army under General Lao Yao-hsiang. Both these general officers had proved themselves as capable commanders during the 1942 campaign. The Chinese formation was given the designation 'X' Force and was sent into Northern Burma in March 1944 where it performed well. At the same time as 'X' Force was being trained in India another force was being trained in Yunnan province. The force received similar but not as extensive training as the troops in India and by 1944 had reached a strength of 100,000 men with the designation 'Y' Force. 'Y' Force was sent westwards from Yunnan into Burma to eventually link up with 'X' Force in January 1945 who had advanced eastward from India.

In this still from a Wartime Newsreel the cameraman has taken a close-up of soldiers who had undergone training at Ramgarh. The men have been newly issued with khaki shirt and shorts and British army webbing equipment. Many of the trainees were young as is shown by the anxious looking soldier in the foreground of the photograph.

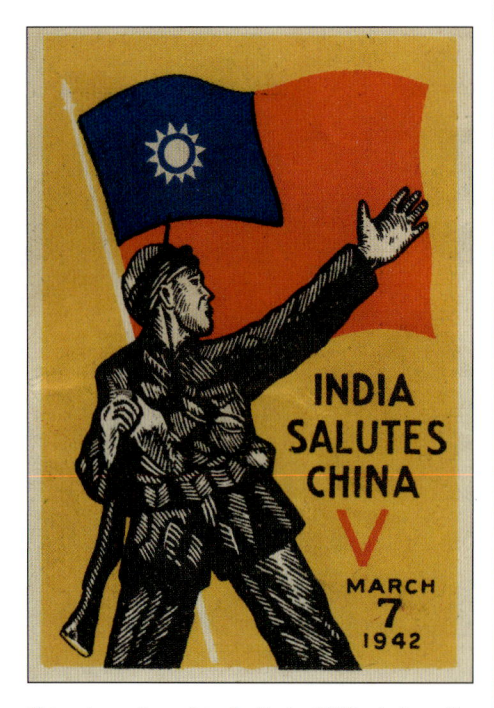

This stamp issued in India in 1942 pledges the government of India to support China in its mutual fight against the Japanese. The pro-Independence Indian National Congress had supported the Chinese cause since 1937. Now in 1942 with the Japanese invasion of British territories like Burma and Malaya the British Empire now had to show support for its Chinese Allies.

Freshly trained soldiers of 'X' Force parade at Ramgarh training camp in late-1942 dressed in their new uniforms and armed with Allied supplied rifles. The men have been issued with khaki drill shirts and shorts and British MKI steel helmets with camouflage netting on them. Although all the men have been given either P-17 rifles or Thompson sub-machine guns the line of U.S. supplied M2A1 105mm howitzers is most impressive. The Chinese Army was desperate for any modern weaponry but the howitzers would have been particularly appreciated.

Allied Training Centres: Ramgarh and Yunnan, 1942-1943

In October 1942 a truck full of Chinese recruits at Ramgarh in India are transported to the firing range in the back of a U.S. truck towing a U.S. supplied 155mm howitzer. The 155mm Howitzer M1918 was originally a French Schneider gun supplied to the U.S. Expeditionary Force in France in 1917. Pneumatic tyres had been added to the original guns as well as a new breech mechanism and there were still over 2,000 in U.S. service in 1940 and some were donated to the Chinese 'X' Force in 1942.

A U.S. instructor at Ramgarh looks down the barrel of his Chinese pupil's Enfield P-17 rifle to check that it has been cleaned properly. Large numbers of the P-17 were supplied to the Chinese by the Allies and it became the standard rifle of the U.S. trained divisions. In an attempt to produce a rifle more suited to the Chinese soldier, 18,000 of the rifles were experimentally altered. They had four inches cut off the barrel with the sights reset and part of the butt also shaved off to produce a more compact rifle.

Two young trainee soldiers practice their semaphore signalling at the Ramgarh Training Centre in India in 1943. The U.S. instructors of the 'Signal Communications Section' were amongst the first personnel to arrive at Ramgarh. These men are sending messages to their U.S. NCO instructors who are checking them for both accuracy and speed. Chinese pupils were also given instruction by the section in radio and field telephone operation and maintenance.

121

Soldiers of the White Sun

During a dress parade at a training camp "somewhere in India" in June 1943 the colour guard of a newly trained and equipped unit lead a column of troops. These young soldiers have been issued with the usual mix of U.S. and British uniforms and equipment. Their flags are not the traditional Nationalist regimental type but are simply the national flag.

Above: Two trainee artillerymen undergo field training on their 75mm M1-A1 pack howitzer and have camouflaged their caps. As well as receiving instruction on how to handle the gun they were also given instruction in how to load them onto mules for transportation.

In September 1943 a U.S. instructor watches on as a 75mm M1-A1 pack howitzer crew receive instruction from his Chinese former pupils. The idea being that the American advisors train the first batch of Chinese trainees who then go on to train further groups of soldiers. To many American's surprise the average Chinese soldier could be trained to operate the 75mm in only a week!

The same artillery crew fire their pack howitzer from cover as they learn from their U.S. instructors how to use the terrain they would encounter in Burma. Most of the M1-A1's supplied to the Chinese after 1942 were mounted older carriages with wooden wheels.

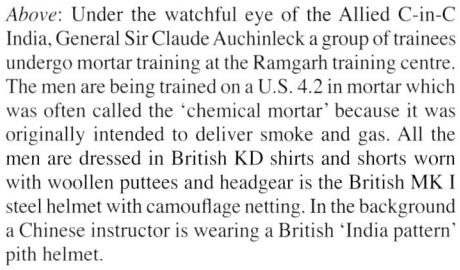

Allied Training Centres: Ramgarh and Yunnan, 1942-1943

Above: Under the watchful eye of the Allied C-in-C India, General Sir Claude Auchinleck a group of trainees undergo mortar training at the Ramgarh training centre. The men are being trained on a U.S. 4.2 in mortar which was often called the 'chemical mortar' because it was originally intended to deliver smoke and gas. All the men are dressed in British KD shirts and shorts worn with woollen puttees and headgear is the British MK I steel helmet with camouflage netting. In the background a Chinese instructor is wearing a British 'India pattern' pith helmet.

Right
Top: Trainees at Ramgarh have target practice under the guidance of a Chinese instructor who has previously been trained by U.S. personnel. The first U.S. instructors started to arrive at Ramgarh in July 1942, just before their first Chinese pupils. By September 1942 all the 9,000 Chinese troops who had been withdrawn from the Burmese theatre were under training at Ramgarh. About 5,000 of them belonged to the 38th Division, while 2,500 were from the 22nd Division. Another 1,200 were from mixed units of the 5th Corps with the remainder coming in small groups from the 96th, 200th and 28th Divisions.

Bottom: U.S. trained and equipped soldiers are pictured on a route march near their training camp in India in November 1943 in preparation for the invasion of Northern Burma. The men are on a twenty-mile march under the instruction of Brigadier-General Haydon. L. Boatner of the U.S. Army who is described in the caption as one of the most colourful characters in the CBI theatre. Boatner who was from San Antonio Texas was said to have a good relationship with both his Chinese pupils and the local Indian population. All these soldiers have been issued with M2 steel helmets, British webbing and they are armed with U.S. Thompson sub-machine guns, P-17 rifles and 60mm M2 mortars.

Soldiers of the White Sun

A truck full of happy trainees of 'Y' or Yoke Force give the thumbs up signal to the photographer as they make their way to the training ground. 'Y Force' was the name given to the Chinese units which received training from a U.S. training mission in Yunnan Province from 1943. Because of supply problems the Chinese troops trained in Yunnan did not receive as good a food ration as their comrades who were being trained in India. Limited as the food may have been it was still a great improvement on what they would have received at the frontline in Burma or Western China.

Two young 'Y Force' trainees in 1943 learn to operate a Danish Madsen light machine gun mounted on its tripod. The Madsen in its various models was one of the many models of machine gun in service with the Chinese Army between 1931-1945. Y Force had to rely to a far greater extent on the equipment and weaponry that it could obtain locally.

WESTERN CHINA, 1943-1944

Above: Soldiers of the newly trained 'Y' Force on the Central Salween River Front cross a river near to the frontline on the 23rd of June 1943. Chinese forces along the Salween River in 1943 amounted to eleven Divisions of 'Y' Force facing the 56th Division of the Imperial Japanese Army. These soldiers described in the caption as 'crack' troops have camouflaged themselves for the river crossing and are armed with FN30 Belgian made carbines.

Right: From this hill top machine gun position these soldiers of 'Y' Force can look down on the winding Salween River and across at the Japanese positions on the opposite bank. The photograph taken in June 1943 shows the kind of terrain in which both sides had to fight during the 1943-1945 campaigns in this region. The Salween River region was one of the three worst Malarial areas in the world and the Chinese soldier suffered terribly during the campaign. One Division began its campaign with 7,000 men and only three weeks later there were only 4,000 of its men fit to fight. In the foreground the officer looks for targets for his ZB-26 machine gunner while the rest of the squad prepare to support with their Mauser Kar.98k rifles.

Soldiers of the White Sun

This still taken from a U.S. Army newsreel of the period shows a close-up of young soldiers on the Salween Front in June 1943. The newsreel shows these and other soldiers firing off round after round from their Mauser short rifles in the general direction of the Japanese who are way out of range. They have also attached foliage to their field caps which bear the usual Nationalist sun cap badge on the front.

In this heavily re-touched photograph a unit fire off a few rounds from their Mauser carbines towards the distant Japanese positions in June 1943. Chinese troops clung to their defence lines until they were ready to launch their offensive in the following year.

Soldiers watch the bombardment of Japanese positions along the Salween River from the shelter of their roughly dug out trenches. The soldiers cotton uniforms are a very light khaki and they have the improvised back packs which are held together with string.

Western China, 1943-1944

An officer wearing a light coloured uniform leads his camouflaged men to take up a new position on the top of a peak in the hills overlooking the Salween River. The Chinese and Japanese faced each other from hill top positions like this in an uneasy stalemate until 1944.

A Chinese Major-General and his aide-de-camp are given a guided tour of the U.S. Army's Aberdeen proving ground. The two officers are members of the Chinese Military Mission and are being shown an 8-inch howitzer by Lieutenant Guy. H. Drewry. These modern heavy guns produced from 1942 were never offered to the Chinese Army as they were desperately needed by the U.S. Army themselves.

This iconic poster painted by Martha Sawyers in support of United China Relief in the U.S. in 1943 makes its point well. It tells the American public that before Pearl Harbor in December 1941, China had already been fighting the Japanese for four years. The troubled relationship between the Allied Powers and the Chinese government during the war meant that their support for Chiang Kai-shek's war effort was conditional.

Soldiers of the White Sun

Young recruits undergo basic instruction on the M24 heavy machine gun in a training camp in Yunnan province in 1944. The men are wearing simple uniforms of roughly made cotton caps, shirts and shorts which some wear with cotton puttees around their lower legs. Two of the men in the background have managed to acquire homemade raffia sun hats with one for some reason having two.

U.S. Army instructor Lieutenant Gene Becker runs his pupils through anti-tank training with their British supplied Boyes anti-tank rifles. The training is taking place at an Allied training camp in Kumming Province, Western China in April 1944. Lieutenant Becker's Instructions are being passed to the trainees by a Chinese Army interpreter. Although obsolete by 1944 the Boyes was certainly still capable of damaging most thinly armoured Japanese light tanks.

In this photograph dated the 28th of July 1944 a U.S. Army Instructor checks the accuracy of his Chinese pupil on a map reading course. The course is taking place at one of the infantry training centres in Western China and is under the overall command of Brigadier-General Thomas. S. Arms. The six weeks Infantry course was open to officers only who would then hopefully pass on their newly learned skills to their men when they returned to their units.

Artillery officers receive training at an unspecified training centre in Western China in 1944. The officer on the right watches for the fall of shot from his artillery battery while his comrades look on. Well-trained officers like these men would form the backbone of the Nationalist Army during the 1946-1949 Civil War.

Western China, 1943-1944

Above: A U.S. instructor at a training facility in Western China gives Chinese chemical troops a lesson in what appears to be the operation of an improvised flamethrower. Some of the trainees seem more interested in the cameraman than in watching the instructor. In most cases however the Chinese troops made good pupils and were often described by their instructors as quick learners.

Right: A 75mm PACK howitzer battery is on mules transported down a gully near to the Field Artillery Training Centre at Kunming in April 1945. Artillery in the Chinese Nationalist Army was at a premium and these gunners would soon be called into action in Burma. The pack on the mule in the foreground carried picks and shovels for digging the gun into position as well as a section of the howitzer.

The Burmese Front, 1944-1945

Chinese Armies on the northern Burma Front in 1944-1945 fought as part of the Allied force who faced the Japanese 33rd Army. The Nationalist 30th and 38th Divisions of 'X' Force known as the New 1st Army formed the left wing of the Allied force which was advanced southward from India taking the strategic airfield of Myitkhina after a siege in August 1944. They next moved to take the town of Bhamo which fell on the 15th of December while at the same time the New 6th Army (50th Division) infiltrated behind Japanese lines to threaten their lines of communication. Beginning in May 'Y' Force had advanced westward from Yunnan province through mountainous terrain with its 53rd and 54th Armies aiming for Teng-Chung on the road to Myitkhina. At the same time its 2nd and 71st Armies were to advance towards Lung-ling in the direction of Bhamo. The overall plan was for 'X' moving southeastward and 'Y' Force moving northwestward to link up and re-open the vital Ledo Road. After months of fighting the link up between 'X' and 'Y' Forces took place on the 21th of January 1945 at Hsipaw on the Ledo Road. The opening of the Ledo Road fulfilled Chiang Kai-shek's main objective for his troops involvement in Burma and he ordered their advance to halt at Lashio which fell on the 7th of March. This angered the U.S. and British commanders who felt that China's role in the Burma Campaign had always been half hearted. However Chiang wanted the elite troops of 'X' and 'Y' Force back in China as soon as possible where they would be needed in the coming conflict with the Communists.

Above: Lieutenant-General Liao Yao-hsiang, the commander of the 22nd Division was rated as one of the best Chinese commanders. Born in 1906 he had attended the Whampoa military academy and then received further military education at the famous St Cyr military academy in France. He was judged by the U.S. advisors as, "A good field soldier, courageous and determined" who followed scrupulously the training directives which had been given to him. By keeping strictly to the U.S. training programme he had built his 22nd Division up to the level of the 'elite' 38th Division regarded as the best Chinese Division.

Right
Top: General Ho Ying-chin, the Chief of the General Staff inspects troops stood in front of a poster bearing Sun Yat-sen's image. As Chiang Kai-shek's deputy in 1945, Ho accepted the surrender of the Japanese forces in China in Nanking. He was a commander of the Eastern Route Army of the National Revolutionary Army during the Northern Expedition of 1926.

Bottom: General Sun Li-Jen commanding officer of the Chinese 38th Division is pictured in late April 1944 in discussion with Colonel Henry Kinnison and General F.D. Merrill of the famous Merrill's Marauders. They are discussing the planned assault against the Japanese held Myitkyina Airfield in Burma. Sun Li-Jen was one of the most able of all Chinese Generals and earned the great respect of his Allies in Burma.

The Burmese Front, 1944-1945

THE SALWEEN RIVER FRONT, 1944

Above: Chinese soldiers of Y-Force re-cross the River Salween in Burma in inflatable dinghy's on the 11th-12th May 1944 under the direct command of the Expeditionary Corps C-in-C General Wei Li-huang. They then went on to capture the Japanese held positions of Kao-li-Kung-Shan, Tung-Chung and Lungling.

Right: General Wei Li-huang directs his army's artillery fire during the fighting on the Salween River Front in June 1944. General Wei born in 1897 had previously been Commander in Chief of the 1st War Area from 1937 to 1942. He then went on to command the Chinese Expeditionary Force from 1942 until 1944 when he was promoted to the position of Deputy Commander in Chief of all Nationalist Forces.

Soldiers of the White Sun

Soldiers of the 2nd Nationalist Army, part of Y-Force fire their Browning M1917 medium machine gun from the shelter of a tree lined bunker on the Salween Front. The 2nd, 71st, 53rd and 54th Armies that made up Y-Force had a strength of 72,000 men and had crossed the Salween River on the night of the 11th of May 1944. Although not as well trained as X-Force, the arms and equipment supplied by the U.S. still made them as elite formation of the Nationalist Army.

General Sun Li-Jen commanding officer of the Chinese 38th Division attended the Virginia Military institute in the United States. He was one of the few Chinese officers respected by Stilwell with whom he had a good working relationship.

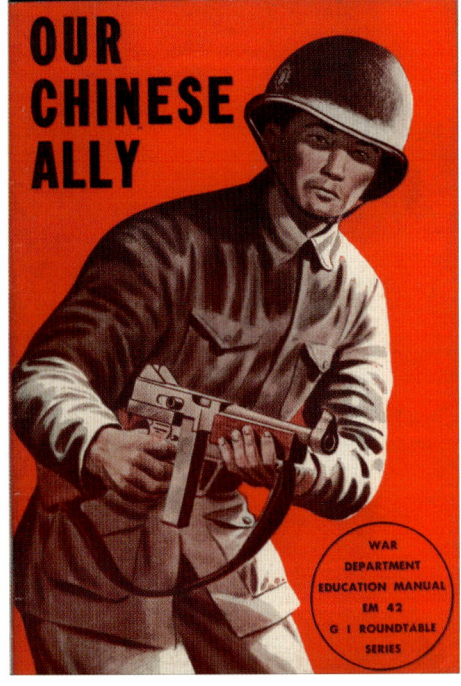

The smiling crewman of a U.S. 75mm PACK howitzer poses proudly with his weapon which was one of the most common types of field gun in service with the Chinese in the 1940s. The PACK howitzer was air transportable and its lightweight construction meant that it could be more easily manhandled by its crew. A shortage of field artillery was always a problem for the Nationalists and individual commanders tended to hoard what they had at their headquarters.

The U.S. soldiers were constantly being educated by their army's information services about their wartime allies and the countries they were fighting in. This cover from a War Department Education Manual from 1943 gives an idealised picture of 'Our Chinese Ally'. In the booklet was information for the American soldier on the culture of the Chinese people and the position that the Nationalist Army had in society. Hopefully this information would help the American GI to understand his allies better and avoid any confrontations caused by misunderstandings.

The Burmese Front, 1944-1945

A U.S. advertisement from 1944 issued by the Superior Steel Corporation of Pennsylvania symbolises the unity between the Allied Powers. It extols the bravery, tenacity and toughness of the British, American, Soviet and Chinese soldiers. Unusually for Allied propaganda it ranks the Chinese Army on the same level as the other armies fighting against the Axis powers.

An immoblised T-26 Model 1933 tank is dug into a defensive position on the Burmese Front as an improvised pillbox. The tanks 47mm main armament would still be capable of causing damage to any Japanese tank in the theatre.

A Soviet supplied T-26 Model 1933 light tank serving with the Chinese Nationalist Army in November 1944. This tank is one of the survivors from over eighty that were supplied to the Chinese by the Soviet Union in 1938.

Left: This Chinese sentry is standing guard over a section of the Burma road sometime during 1944. His uniform is a confusing mixture of summer and winter items with a wadded cotton jacket worn with summer weight trousers and woollen puttees. The helmet appears to be a French Adrian model which was worn most often by soldiers from the southwest of China. He is well equipped with a backpack and has two 'potato masher' grenades worn in pouches on either side of his chest and he is armed with a Mauser carbine.

Soldiers of the White Sun

Artillerymen prepare to move towards the front in 1944 with their 75mm PACK howitzers disassembled so that their mules can pull them. The mules would have to transport the guns as well as the shells and all the other equipment needed by the unit. Some of the men have been issued with French Adrian helmets with the Nationalist sun emblem on the front. Personnel equipment varies from man to man with the two men in the left foreground have bamboo-framed backpacks on.

A smiling Artilleryman from a 75mm PACK howitzer unit poses with one of the mules being used to transport the unit's guns in Burma. The difficult terrain in Northern Burma meant that the Allies had to rely heavily on animal transport and each division had about 1,000 mules or horses. Keeping this large number of animals fed was a constant problem and forage for them was often supplied by airdrop. In this photograph dated the 29th of February 1944 the soldier wears the usual mix of Allied supplied uniform, equipment and weaponry. His helmet, pullover and webbing are supplied from British stores in India but the P-17 rifle comes from U.S. sources.

A smiling seven-year-old Private Koo Ho-king of the 39th Division of the 6th Army shoulders more than his fair share of the load during fighting to clear the Burma Road in July 1944. He is part of a unit of boy soldiers who are acting as porters for their older comrades as they move up to the frontline. Although Private Koo has been issued with a smart new uniform he like his fellow boy soldiers is unarmed. When they get to the front they may well be expected to take part in the fighting when a rifle becomes available.

Above: The firer of the export model of the U.S. Browning M1917A1 medium machine gun squints down the sights of his gun in a trench in Burma. Export models of this popular machine gun had spade grips instead of the standard pistol grip and were known as the MG38. This crew has all been issued with the U.S. M2 steel helmet to go with their light khaki cotton uniforms.

Top right: A patrol dressed in a mixture of Allied supplied uniforms and equipment brings in three blindfolded Japanese soldiers during fighting in 1944. The Chinese show a good cross section of what was worn by the Allied supplied troops in Burma. Helmets are mainly British MKI pattern with a few U.S. M1s worn by two of the men and rifles are U.S. supplied P-17s. Even though the men are wearing British KD trousers they have continued the Chinese practice of tucking theirs into their puttees.

Right: The crew of a U.S. supplied M3A1 37mm anti-tank gun bring their gun into action during fighting in North Burma. M3A1s were totally obsolete by 1944 in the European theatre but were still useful in the Pacific theatre. They could be used in the infantry support role firing high explosive rounds but could also destroy the lightly armoured Japanese tanks.

Soldiers advance past the bodies of dead Japanese during their advance through a Northern Burmese village. The men are all armed with the P-17 rifle and have been issued with U.S. M2 helmets.

Soldiers of the White Sun

BATTLE OF TENG-CHUNG, 1944

Right: In the midst of the bitter fighting for Teng-Chung this Thompson sub-machine gunner fires his weapon from behind a sandbagged barricade. The Nationalist 8th Army attacked Teng-Chung and the nearby town of Sung-Shan in August 1944.

Above: Moving through the ruins of Teng-Chung a flamethrower operator prepares to fire his U.S. supplied M1-A1. First introduced in 1942 in the U.S. Army the M1-A1 was only issued to the Chinese Army in limited numbers. It was replaced in the U.S. Army by the improved M2-A2 after 1944 but the Chinese would have been happy to receive the older model.

Right: A ZB-26 light machine gun crew fire their weapon from behind an improvised barricade in the battle for the walled city of Teng-Chung in Western Yunnan province. The attack on the 14th of September 1944 succeeded in taking the city on the 15th but this did not as intended lead to the re-opening of the Burma Road.

Right: General Stilwell pins an award to the first in a line of soldiers in a clearing in the Burmese Jungle. Stilwell was proud of the Chinese soldiers under his command and had a great deal of affection for the rank and file. His relationship with many of the higher-ranking officers was not so cordial and he openly despised some of them. He particularly hated the abuses inflicted on long suffering Chinese soldiers by some of their officers. At the same time he recognised that there were other officers like General Sun Li-jen who genuinely cared for their men's welfare.

The Burmese Front, 1944-1945

Left: During fighting for Teng-Chung, in November 1944 a first aid station is set up in the street to treat the wounded. Although the average Chinese soldier was used to having to put up with poor treatment the lack of medical care for these wounded men is pitiful. The relative indifference of a passer by to the plight of his fellow countrymen is also symptomatic of a people who had grown used to seeing this kind of suffering.

Below: A Major of the Nationalist 22nd Division in Burma shows a U.S. signal liaison officer, Captain F.J. Holmes a piece of shrapnel which just missed him when at the frontline. In the background is a regimental flag of the Japanese Imperial Army's 18th Division which was captured by the 22nd at Walla Bum. The Major is wearing a rough cotton khaki tunic which appears to be an other ranks issue and he also wears a battered U.S. steel helmet. He is also holding a U.S. M2 carbine which is an unusual weapon for an high ranking officer to be armed with.

Left: Happy Chinese soldiers of the 22nd Division wait patiently for their turn to be transported back to China over the Himalayas in the U.S. Air Force C-47 transport planes behind them. The men are armed with U.S. supplied P-17 rifles with the man on the right having an M9A1 anti-tank grenade launcher fitted on his. On the ground in front of several of the young soldiers are folded U.S. 60mm M2 mortars. These men are part of the force of 25,105 Chinese soldiers, 249 American personnel, 1,596 horses and mules, forty-two 1/4-ton trucks, forty-eight 75mm. Howitzers, forty-eight 4.2-inch mortars and forty-eight 37mm anti-tank guns flown over the hump between the 22nd December 1944 and the 5th of January 1945!

137

Soldiers of the White Sun

The Burmese Front, 1944-1945

Above

Left: Using a primitive and labour intensive method Chinese soldiers assist in the refuelling of a U.S. A.T.C. transport plane with jerry cans. Chinese troops and thousands of Indian labourers were pressed into service on U.S. airfields

Right: A ten-year-old boy soldier is a member of a Chinese division which is being airlifted from the North Airstrip at Myitkyina in Burma to China on the 5th of December 1944. He is fully kitted out with the MK1 steel helmet with netting and KD shirt and shorts and also has a couple of canvas bags on his hips. His older comrade in the background has a U.S. M2 steel helmet and carries his kit slung from either end of a pole.

Opposite

Top: These troops sat in neat rows with their packs laid out before them are waiting for permission to get aboard the C-47 behind them. Chinese units were air transported into Burma from training centres in Yunnan Province and from Ramgarh in India back to China. The units primitive cooking pot is stacked next to them showing they will have to rely on their own resources when in the field.

Bottom: Petrified soldiers sit rigidly as they are being flown back to China in one of the U.S. Air Force's transport planes. The U.S.-A.T.C. (Air Transport Command) moved thousands of Chinese troops from theatre to theatre during the war. For instance between the 1st April and 11th May 1944 they transported the 6th Army's 25,136 men, 2,178 horses and 1,565 tons of equipment to assist in the defence of Chungking.

Chinese forces of the 38th Division fire from their trenches amidst the local temples on the outskirts of Bhamo as they try and take the town in November 1944. Fighting around the important town continued into 1945 with the Japanese sending 3,000 reinforcements in to bolster its defence in December 1944.

Soldiers of the White Sun

This photograph taken by a U.S. Army photographer in December 1944 is of a Browning M1917A1 machine gun crew near the town of Bhamo. After the taking of Myitkina by the Chinese New 1st Army and Allied troops in August 1944 the next objective as they advanced southwards Bhamo which was situated on the Irrawaddy River. The town was largely surrounded by the Chinese 38th Division in early-November but it was unable to take it.

Opposite
Top: Looking like something from a bygone age a howitzer crew's mules pull their gun along the Burma Road in 1944. The ramshackle way that the crew's kit and equipment have been piled onto the gun and its limber does not give the impression of a well organised unit. This gun is an ex-Soviet 4.5 inch MKI howitzer which had originally been supplied to Tsarist Russia by its British manufacturers during World War I. A few of these surplus guns were then sent by Russia to China as part of the arms shipments of the late-1930s.

Bottom: Abandoned at the side of a Japanese pillbox at Chefang in 1945 this immobilised Italian made CV-33 tankette is a relic of China's recent military past. How this lightly armoured two man light tank survived until 1945 it is hard to say as most of the other vehicles of its type were destroyed in the fighting of 1937-1938. The CV-33 was totally outclassed by all other armoured vehicles as early as 1940 so five years later it would be regarded as a museum piece.

A soldier of the Chinese forces trained in India takes aim with his P-17 rifle on the Northern Burma front. His U.S. supplied M2 steel helmet and British supplied Indian Army pullover illustrate how the Chinese soldier on the Burmese front was jointly equipped and clothed by the Allies.

A mortar crew fire their U.S. M1 81mm from the shelter of the dense Burmese jungle in 1944. The mortar is the U.S. version of the Stokes-Brandt M-1927/31 and was supplied to the Chinese in large quantities. Two of the crewmen wear the India pattern pith helmet which was issued to the Chinese in India in small numbers.

The Burmese Front, 1944-1945

Soldiers of the White Sun

Left: Soldiers of the Chinese Expeditionary Force receive instruction in operating the U.S. supplied 2.36in M1 rocket launcher commonly known as the 'bazooka' in 1945. The bazooka could penetrate armour up to about four inches and could easily deal with any Japanese tank encountered in Burma in 1944-1945. This lightweight weapon could also be used against concrete emplacements and in street fighting. It would be a useful weapon for the Chinese as they advanced into the cities of Burma during 1945.

Above: A U.S. issued poster from the U.S. News Agency from 1944 symbolises the hoped for friendship between the Chinese soldier and his American advisor who wears the CBI arm badge. The Chinese characters on the poster read, "Brother In Arms to Defeat Japanese Bandits." Many U.S. advisors did have a great deal of respect for the ordinary Chinese soldier who was often a willing pupil. They often did not however have the same respect for the high ranking Chinese officers many of who mistreated their men.

Above: Soldiers cross the Shweli River on a local boat near the town of Namkham in Northern Burma on the 16th of January 1945. These men of the Nationalist New 1ST Army had captured the town on the previous day in their rapid advance through North Burma in the first weeks of 1945. The Japanese had been surprised that the Chinese had continued their advance once they had crossed the China-Burmese border. Rivers were a constant obstacle to any advance in Burma, and this primitive form of river crossing was often the only way to get across.

Right: Soldiers prepare to move their PACK howitzers across the Shweli River during the advance against the Japanese. The howitzers have been broken down into their component parts and then will be loaded onto rafts to take them across the river.

The Burmese Front, 1944-1945

Above: During the advance on the strategic town of Lashio in March 1945, Chinese Artillery units had to move their howitzers across swollen streams. The bridges across the rivers and streams in the area have been destroyed by the retreating Japanese. In this case a U.S. bulldozer is having to drag a U.S. supplied truck and the 155mm M918 howitzer it is towing out of the mud watched by disinterested soldiers. Piled in the back of the truck is the personal gear of the gun crew as well as wooden crates of shells for the howitzer.

Below: M3A3 'Stuart' light tanks of the 3rd Battalion, Chinese Provisional Tank Group, advance across a stream in Northern Burma. The Provisional Tank Group was raised initially in 1943 as part of 'X' Force in India and earned a good reputation in its first actions in 1944. Although classed as a light tank the M3A3 was more than capable of taking on any armour that the Japanese had in Burma at the time.

Soldiers of the White Sun

Above
Left: In this close up of a M3A3 light tank of the Provisional Tank Group in 1944 we can see that all of the crew are Chinese. When the unit first went into action the crews of the tanks were a mixture of Chinese and U.S. instructors. As soon as the Chinese crews had proven their competency the Americans were switched back into a support and training role. Chinese tank crews received barely three months training and learned to operate their tanks in a remarkably short time. This is particularly surprising when you consider that none of the trainees had driven any type of motorised transport before.

Right: A Sherman M4A4 medium tank of the Chinese Army's 1st Provisional Tank Group is crossing the Nam Yao River during the units attack on Lashio on the 6th of March 1945. The lead tank is negotiating a shallow part of the river while the rest of the column advances down the slope. Sherman's were certainly a potent weapon in the fighting in Burma especially when you consider the poor state of the Japanese armour that they might face. The Provisional Tank Group was equipped with M3A3 Stuart light tanks and Universal Carriers from Allied Lend Lease stocks in India to compliment the Shermans.

Left: This Sherman M4A4 medium tank is painted in standard U.S. Army khaki finish with the gaudy addition of a wildcat's face and outstretched claw. The Sherman with a main armament of a 75mm gun and with three Browning machine guns was a formidable tank. Particularly when compared with the poorly armoured Japanese tanks that were in Burma in 1944-1945.

Right: Young crewmen of a Sherman M4A4 pose in their tank for an U.S. Army photographer before going into action in March 1945. As you might expect their tank overalls and crash helmets are U.S. Army issue to go with their U.S. supplied tank. Most Chinese crewmen came from rural backgrounds with little previous exposure to modern machinery. According to their U.S. instructors their lack of experience did not stop them from quickly learning to operate the Shermans.

Below: Tank '313' of the 1st Provisional Tank Group speeds through a Burmese village near Lashio in March 1945. The crew are obviously not expecting to meet Japanese resistance as they are all out of their hatches and their gun has a dust cover over it. On the front of the Sherman M4A4 is painted the face of a wildcat which may have been particular to this tank.

The Chinese Homefront, 1944-1945

The war on the mainland of China in 1944 was dominated by the launch of the Japanese ICHIGO – 'Number One' – offensive in April. This large-scale offensive involved 400,000 Japanese troops in seventeen divisions with 12,000 motor vehicles, 1,500 artillery pieces, 800 tanks and 70,000 horses. It was the largest operation launched by the Japanese during the Sino-Japanese War and was intended to destroy U.S. airbases throughout central China. The offensive was launched through Honan, Hupeh and Hunan provinces and carried all before it. A 390,000 strong Chinese Army tried to halt the Japanese advance at Loyang in May and held it back for twelve days. Most Chinese forces were able to withdraw in front of the Japanese and it was the civilian population that suffered most with estimates of 200,000 dead. When the offensive petered out in December 1944 the amount of Chinese territory under Japanese control had been substantially increased. In addition many airbases operated by the 14th and 20th U.S. air forces along with their personnel had been evacuated ahead of the offensive. The success of ICHIGO did not however alter the course of the war and by early-1945 the Japanese began to withdraw from some regions of China. During April-May 1945 the Japanese launched one last offensive towards the U.S. airbase at Chihchiang which was halted by the Chinese. With the war situation in the Pacific deteriorating the Japanese spent the rest of the summer of 1945 in China gearing down their war effort.

Below: In a photograph dated 28th of April 1944 the 19th Division is seen on parade wearing another variation on the standard Chinese uniform. Although well equipped and uniformed compared to most Chinese units this Division has a mixture of sources of supply. The helmets are the French Adrian model M1915 which were originally copied by the Chinese in 1930 in small numbers. In this case as the 19th Division was supplied by the U.S. government so they may have come from stores of helmets provided for the American Expeditionary Force in 1917. If that is the case they have been refurbished and given the Nationalist sun emblem on the front. Arms appear to be from Belgian sources with FN1930 short rifles and the FN Mle-30 heavy automatic rifles. Equipment includes U.S. canvas ammunition belts and backpacks which could have been provided from a variety of sources.

The Chinese Homefront, 1944-1945

Left: A heavy machine gun crew fire their Czechoslovakian made ZB VZ/53 from behind a concrete embrasure on the Yellow River Front in January 1944. The VZ/53 was one of the more reliable weapons of its type in service with the Chinese in World War II and was originally imported at the same time as the ZB26 light machine gun. Lend lease supplies of small arms were never sufficient to allow the replacement of weaponry bought by China in the 1930s.

Below: Artillerymen of the 2nd Army fire their 75mm PACK howitzer M1A1 from a dug in position on the Southern China Front in Spring 1944. This gun is on the M1 type carriage which had metal wheels with spokes rather than the later M8 type which had tires. The range of the M1A1 was 8930 metres which compared well with its Japanese equivalent, the Type 94 which had a range of 8178 metres.

A column of soldiers march through a village while campaigning in South China in the Spring of 1944. Chinese troops were often not welcome in their own countryside as they had the habit of looting and taking goods without paying. The ordinary Chinese peasantry had suffered from the bad behaviour of their soldiers for centuries. This problem was always more acute when the soldiers moving through a region were from another part of China. Soldiers fighting away from their own province often had little regard for the feelings of the population.

A home guardsman stands guard at a barracks at Pihu Training Centre in Fukien Province in 1944. He is dressed in a rather unkempt wadded cotton jacket and is wearing what appears to be a U.S. World War I model steel helmet. His equipment is pretty basic with a couple of canvas ammunition bandoliers to carry rounds for his Mauser Kar.98k rifle with its fixed bayonet.

Soldiers of the White Sun

Left: The original caption to this U.S. Navy photograph of 1944 says simply 'Chinese 'GI' and shows happy Nationalist soldiers waiting at a railway station. They carry the traditional umbrella which had often been a part of a Chinese soldiers kit for many years. Although the use of umbrellas by Chinese soldiers was often derided by some Westerners they were very practical. When as was normal no tents were available they provided shelter from the rain and in the summer they gave shade from the sun and could be camouflaged to protect against air attack. The man in the centre of the photograph who is armed with a Mauser rifle has a locally made tooled leather belt with two ammunition pouches on each side. This appears to be a crudely made version of the German ammunition belts used by the Chinese during the 1930s.

Armoured troops pass by their commander General Lung Yun the governor of Yunnan Province in October 1944. Their vehicles show the disparate sources of Chinese armour with a German supplied Kfz.221 scout car in front and two U.S. supplied White scout cars behind. The German vehicles were of course sold to China before 1939 while the White armoured cars are more recent acquisitions.

This is an anti-Japanese propaganda leaflet dropped from U.S. planes over the Burmese Front in 1944-1945. A Chinese soldier bayonets the serpent festooned in the Rising Sun of the Japanese Empire. The leaflet emphasises that the Japanese are not yet defeated with the characters state, "A half dead snake can still bite."

This German supplied Kfz.221 scout car in Yunnan Province in 1944 is a survivor from the armoured vehicles that China acquired between 1936-1938. It is still in the Germay field grey colour scheme that it was delivered in and is armed with a MG-34 general purpose machine gun.

The Chinese Homefront, 1944-1945

Above: Smartly uniformed provincial policemen provide a guard of honour for a visiting dignitary in Yunnan Province in 1944. Nationalist China needed a well-armed police force to counter its internal enemies as well as protecting its population from its external ones. The men all have painted French Adrian steel helmets with silver painted combs and have the Nationalist sun stencilled on the front. The white cloth puttees and gloves worn with the light khaki uniform by the other ranks complete their parade dress and they are all armed with Mauser Kar.98k rifles.

Volunteers for the much vaunted 'Youth Force' show their patriotism at a recruitment parade in 1944. In an attempt to rejuvenate the war effort Chiang Kai-shek announced in a speech on the 27th of August 1944 the formation of the force. It was to be raised from the student population of unoccupied China and by November 1944 was reported to be 125,500 strong. The volunteers were organised into nine Youth Divisions and then into three Corps with some of the young men being flown to be trained in India.

Two young soldiers are seen on guard duty on the approach to an airbase of the U.S. 14th Air Force in China in 1944. Behind them looking on are U.S. Army Air Force personnel who have pulled up in their 15 CWT truck. The boys have simple rough cotton uniforms worn with puttees and straw sandals and have their names written on the cloth strips over their breast pockets.

149

Soldiers of the White Sun

Right: General Ch'en Ch'eng born in 1897 is pictured here at the end of the Sino-Japanese War when he was Minister of War. Ch'en has been a graduate of the Paoting Military Academy in 1922 and served the Nationalists first in the Northern Expedition where he commanded first the 27th and then the 11th Divisions. He then went on to command large forces during the extermination campaigns against the Communists and in 1937 was in command of the 3rd War Area. He combined his field commands with his role as Vice Minister of War from 1937 and from 1940 to 1944 he was commander of the 6th War Area. During 1944 he was also commander in chief of the Expeditionary Force and Commander of the 1st War Area before becoming Minister of War in November of that year.

Troops disembark down the gangplank from a naval vessel. The soldier in the foreground appears to be the unit cook, as he carries cooking utensils hanging from his wooden yoke. Directly behind him is a mortar man, and to his rear a machine gunner armed with a ZB-26 and his loader who carries pouches for spare magazines. After Japan's surrender in August 1945, large numbers of Nationalist troops were transported to areas of China previously under Japanese occupation.

This propaganda leaflet from 1945 highlights the danger of 'loose talk costs lives' seen in many World War II posters from all nations. The text says, "There is an ear behind the wall" and then emphasises the message with, "Don't discuss Military Affairs".

Left: A U.S. trained 81mm M1 mortar crew fire their weapon during an offensive against the Japanese in the vicinity of Chihchiang Airbase to the southeast of Chungking in May 1945. The airbase used by the U.S. 14th Air Force came under attack by the Japanese during the previous month. Pressure was taken off the defending Chinese by a series of successful outflanking attacks on the advancing Japanese.

The Chinese Homefront, 1944-1945

Left: Soldiers listen to a speech from a commanding officer in spring 1945 wearing the unusual cloth insignia on their field caps. They are dressed for winter campaigning with wadded cotton jackets and most have the improvised roll packs used as a substitute for traditional haversacks. The men on the far right of the photograph have shovels sticking out of their packs and are most likely the pioneer or engineer platoon of the unit. All are armed with Mauser Kar.98 rifles or one of its foreign derivatives, the Czech VZ24 or the Belgian FN30.

Above: General Cheng Tung-kuo was the commander of the New 1st Army from 1943-1944 and then Deputy Commander of the C.A.I (Chinese Army in India) from 1944. Here he addresses some of his 'elite' troops in Nanning on the 17th of August 1945. Cheng was one of the first graduates of the Whampoa Military Academy in 1924 and went on to command the six Division strong 1st Army in Manchuria during the 1946-1949 Civil War.

Left: Reinforcements march into the newly recaptured city of Kweilin in Kwangsi province and pass the troops that they are relieving. The city was taken on the 27th of July 1945 after falling to the Japanese in November 1944, during their Ichigo offensive. The soldiers in the column are reasonably well equipped and are armed with a mixture of Mauser rifles and ZB-26 machine guns. Their uniforms are the usual cotton shirt and shorts and caps and many of them have either been issued with or have otherwise acquired locally made sun hats.

Left: Well turned out Nationalist troops listen to a 'pep' talk from their commanding officer wearing newly issued winter padded uniforms in late 1945. The Nationalist Army began the Civil War in good spirits with an overwhelming superiority in men and weaponry.

U.S. Training of Chinese Specialist Troops, 1944-1945

Right: At the same Commando School a unit of Chinese volunteers line up for inspection dressed in a more or less uniform manner. They all have the M2 steel helmet and simple cotton tunics and trousers worn without any noticeable insignia. Equipment carried by the men seems to include U.S. pattern canvas belt with cartridge pouch and the officer in the foreground has a binocular case. Most of the men are armed with the Springfield M1903 rifle which a cast off from the U.S. Army but one or two have Thompson sub-machine guns. Resting on the ground in the centre of the unit's squad weapon, a Browning M1919A6 light machine gun.

Below: In this photograph dated the 8th of May 1945 a unit of Chinese volunteers receive training from a U.S. instructor of a Chinese Commando School in Western China. The school run by the, OSS – 'Office of Strategic Services', the forerunner to the CIA – could only train a relatively small number of men. All the Chinese have been kitted out with U.S. M2 steel helmets but otherwise are dressed in a mixture of U.S. fatigues with various types of footwear. On the left of the photograph are what look like a group of N.C.Os who are armed with the M1 carbine while the rest of the men have to make do with the out of date Springfield M1903 rifle.

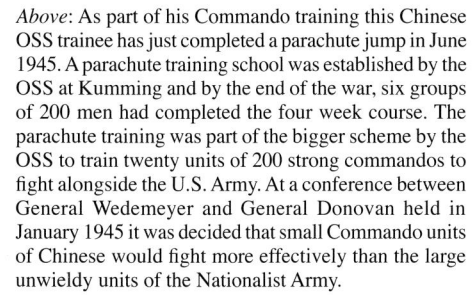

Above: As part of his Commando training this Chinese OSS trainee has just completed a parachute jump in June 1945. A parachute training school was established by the OSS at Kumming and by the end of the war, six groups of 200 men had completed the four week course. The parachute training was part of the bigger scheme by the OSS to train twenty units of 200 strong commandos to fight alongside the U.S. Army. At a conference between General Wedemeyer and General Donovan held in January 1945 it was decided that small Commando units of Chinese would fight more effectively than the large unwieldy units of the Nationalist Army.

Above: A U.S. Army instructor, Lieutenant Claude E. Davis gives training to Chinese guerrillas in Kwangsi Province near Liuchow in July 1945. Limited training programmes provided by the Allies could not really affect the overall performance of the Chinese Army. The vast majority of Chinese soldiers received little or no training and were totally unprepared for what faced them.

Below: Chinese guerrillas are pictured during training by the SACO - Sino-American-Co-operative Organisation in September 1945. In operation in China since 1942 this U.S. Navy task force made up of Naval, Marine and Coastguard instructors was responsible for the training of Chinese troops in all kinds of military skills including as here target practice.

The Surrender of Imperial Japanese Forces in China, September 1945

After the dropping of the atomic bombs on Hiroshima on the 6th of August and on Nagasaki on the 9th, Japan's capitulation was certain. Even before the official surrender broadcast by Emperor Hirohito on the 15th of August Japanese troops in China were withdrawing from the south. The Allied Powers gave Chiang Kai-shek the right to organise the handover of power by the defeated Japanese as he chose. Chiang ordered Japanese units in occupied China to hold their positions until Nationalist units could relieve them. He also requested that the U.S. airlift and move his troops by sea to the north of China to try and forestall a Communist takeover of the region. The movement of Nationalist troops into areas formally under Communist control meant the re-opening of the Civil War. The 1,385,000 Japanese soldiers in China along with 500,000 civilians were prepared for repatriation back to Japan by December 1945 with little retaliation for their brutal occupation.

Right: General Ho Ying-chin on behalf of the National Government receives the surrender of all Japanese troops in China from General Neiji Okamura at 9:00am on the 9th of September 1945. General Ho accepts the surrender text from Okamura on behalf of Chiang Kai-shek in the hall of the Central Military Academy in Nanking. According to the terms of the surrender document there were 1,283,240 Japanese combatants in China at the time of Japan's defeat. With civilians and foreign auxiliaries the total that needed repatriated was over two million.

Below: Local ceremonies like this one took place all over China as all Nationalist commanders of war zones were to accept the surrender of the Japanese troops in their region. This surrender ceremony takes place in a local hall with the large portrait of Sun Yat-sen, the founder of the Kuomintang dominating the proceedings. Overall the surrender of Japanese forces went remarkably smoothly in the areas that came under Nationalist control. The Nationalists main concern was to 'liberate' as much territory as possible before the Communists could move in and set up their own governments.

The Surrender of Imperial Japanese Forces in China, September 1945

Chinese officers and their Japanese counterparts meet to discuss local issues about the handover of control of former occupied territories. Despite the years of bitter conflict between the Japanese and Chinese the surrender of occupying forces and the handover of territory went relatively smoothly. The Nationalist Army's priority was to move reliable units into Japanese occupied China before the Communists could steal a march on them.

A well turned out unit of former puppet soldiers of Wang Ching-wei's pro-Japanese government in Nanking salute their new employers in 1945. The Nationalist Army like the Communists were willing to take into their ranks the ordinary soldiers of the former puppet armies. They provided an already trained source of manpower and many of them were former Nationalist troops anyway. Often Chinese troops when surrounded by the Japanese and cut off from central government had the stark choice of annihilation or a temporary switching of sides. Most of these troops had little or no loyalty to the 'puppet' Wang Ching-wei government and certainly not to the Japanese Imperial Army.

Nationalist officers examine the stockpiles of captured Japanese rifles handed over by surrendering soldiers. Most of the captured Japanese small arms were taken into Chinese service and were used in the Civil War of 1946-1949. The largest stocks were however captured in Manchuria from the Japanese Kwangtung Army by the Soviet Army and handed over to their Chinese Communist allies.

155

CIVIL WAR, 1946-1949

Right: A smartly dressed sentry guards a government building in the city of Tientsin in November 1945. Above the entrance to the building are the crossed flags with the white sun emblem in the centre. The flag on the left of the gates is the 'White Sun in Blue Sky' which is the flag of the Kuomintang Party and was adopted in 1906. On the right of the gate flies the 'White Sun in Blue Sky over Red Ground' flag which was adopted as the flag of the Republic on October 8th 1928. During the Summer and Autumn of 1945 the Nationalists took back as many cities and towns as they could from the Japanese and Communists. One of their first acts when 'liberating' a town was to adorn all public buildings with one or both of these flags.

Below: In March 1946 a rag-tag column of Nationalist troops marches through the streets of Mukden the capital of Manchuria. The men are dressed in winter uniforms with fur hats of various shapes and sizes and one man has a pair of thick gloves. About 50% of the men appear to be unarmed and presumably have to wait to get a rifle from a fallen comrade. According to the original caption for the photograph these men are going to face expected Communist attacks after the sudden withdrawal of the Soviet Unions occupation troops.

Right: Two young Nationalist soldiers stand outside their pillbox which guards the army's headquarters in Mukden in March 1946. Dominating the building is a huge portrait of Chiang Kai-shek whose control of Manchuria was weakening. The age and appearance of the two soldiers does not exactly inspire confidence in the Nationalist's control of this vital city. They both wear padded winter jackets and fur hats but the youngest has also acquired a fur lined sleeveless coat.

Below: Armed police guard their station which is heavily sandbagged in case of trouble as the Soviet troops prepare to leave Mukden in March 1946. Nationalist police acted in a military role when required although their main role was keeping the population in order. As well as the regular police force who were armed, there were two other armed Nationalist police forces, Traffic Police and Railway Police who were both involved in keeping lines of communication open. The two men on guard here are well kitted out for the adverse weather with their fur hats and fur lined boots and both are armed with Mauser rifles.

This and the next two photographs show embarkation of the Nationalist 22nd Division of the New 6th Army at Shanghai. The men are being taken by U.S. Navy ships to Chinwangtao the chief port in the Northern Chinese province of Hopeh. From there they were to be sent into Manchuria to take part in decisive battles with the main Communist formations which would largely decide the fate of the Nationalist cause. In one photograph we can see that each man who is about to embark has been given the responsibility of carrying a bundle of five rifles each. These would presumably be given to soldiers already in the frontline when the men arrived there.

Civil War, 1946-1949

These two photographs show a nursing unit about to embark by sea for the fighting in Manchuria. The young women wear the same uniforms as their male counterparts and have no distinguishing insignia to indicate their role. In the second photograph the only clue to their role as medical staff is the fact that they are sat on first aid boxes on the quay before departure for the front.

Above: A U.S. Marine poses outside a sentry box with a Nationalist guard during the Marine Corps involvement in China. In the immediate aftermath of the Japanese surrender large numbers of U.S. Marines were shipped to North China. Their role was to assist the Nationalists in demobilising the defeated Japanese and their Chinese puppet troops and this involved initially over 50,000 marines. By 1946 their number had been reduced by 50% and by the time the last Marines left China in May 1949 the few that were left had been guarding U.S. nationals.

Left: General Ho Ying-chin is pictured in November 1946 at a military conference in the U.S. where he was stationed until March 1948. In March 1948 he returned to China to serve as Minister of National Defence having served as War Minister during the latter stages of the Second World War.

Soldiers of the White Sun

An ex-Japanese Type 94 'Te-Ke' tankette now in Nationalist service rolls through the streets of Taiyuan the capital of the province of Shansi. Shansi had been under the control of Marshal Yen His-shan 'The Model Governor' since 1911 when he had revolted against the Manchu Emperor. Marshal Yen had survived the 1920s by siding with the victorious Nationalists who took control of China in 1928. He had then fought the Japanese in the 1930s before making accommodations with them in the late-1930s and early-1940s. There was no way that he could survive the repeated Communist attacks on his province even though he defeated their assaults in 1948 and into 1949. He had vowed to take cyanide rather than surrender his power he eventually escaped to Nanking in 1949 taking his gold reserve with him. Yen's Army was quite well trained and equipped and included a 4,000 man Japanese volunteer force after 1945. The Japanese troops in his army are reported to have fought against the Communists to the last man when they took the capital.

Below: Nationalist artillerymen are pictured outside their ramshackle barracks in Yingpan with a 75mm PACK howitzer in November 1947. The men are wearing padded light khaki uniforms with U.S. type peaked caps worn by the Nationalists after 1946. Although the Nationalists did have heavier U.S. supplied 105 and 155mm howitzers the vast majority of their guns were of this type.

Posing outside his walled garrison in Shansi Province in 1947 this Nationalist boy soldier wears a primitively made peaked cap with crudely made badge on the front. The cap has been modelled on a U.S. type peaked cap which were issued to the Nationalist Army in large numbers. He is armed with a 'war booty' Arisaka 38 rifle and he has its bayonet in its scabbard on his left hip. The rest of his rag-tag uniform is made up of rough light khaki cotton shirt and trousers and he has canvas bandoliers over his shoulder and around his waist.

Civil War, 1946-1949

Right: A lone guard holding a Thompson sub-machine from the 38th Nationalist Division watches over a group of Communist captives in the winter of 1947. The 38th were one of the two Divisions trained by the Allies at Ramgarh during the Second World War. As such this veteran of the fighting in Burma in 1944-1945 would be battle hardened and would certainly be a match for the best of the Communist armies. All of the men in the photograph wear the same basic padded cotton winter uniform and would only be distinguished by the insignia on their hats.

Below: In this photograph from March 1947, General Wei Li-huang poses for U.S. newsmen on a tour of an American tank factory. General 'Hundred Victories' Wei had earned his nickname during the campaigns against the Communists in the early-1930s. He would soon be back in China taking command of the Nationalist forces in Manchuria from October this year. The Nationalists constantly pleaded for more U.S. heavy weaponry like the tank behind the General to defeat the Communists. Many in the U.S. Congress were however rapidly becoming disillusioned with the performance of Chang Kai-shek's forces. They began to believe that sending tanks, artillery and other weaponry to the Nationalists was aiding the Communists who captured large amounts of it from their enemies.

Right center: During a parade held in Shanghai in 1947 these well turned out soldiers of a Nationalist Youth Division shout patriotic slogans loudly for the press. The Youth Divisions formed from amongst the more pro-Nationalist students were still full of 'revolutionary' spirit even of only for the cameras. All the young men have 'war booty' M32 Japanese helmets on with Nationalist emblems attached to the front. Their uniforms are made from light khaki cotton and they have a basic kit of a canvas bread bag. They are fortunate to have all been issued with U.S. supplied double-buckle boots which would have been a rarity in the Nationalist Army of 1947.

Right: This heavy machine gun crew of the Nationalist Army are wearing the new 'Model 1946' winter uniforms. It was wrongly assumed that this new type of centrally produced uniform followed the previous pattern of winter issue clothing by being made from blue grey cloth. In fact it appears that the vast majority of suits of winter tunics, trousers and hats were made in a yellowish khaki colour. However in the chaotic situation in China at the time probably meant that some were produced in a grey colour. We can see on the man on the left of the photograph the neat recesses in the earflaps of the winter hat that fitted around the wearers ear. The heavy machine gun used by the crew is a Type-24 which was produced in several Chinese arsenals as a copy of the German Maxim M1908.

161

Soldiers of the White Sun

A Nationalist medium machine gun crew sheltering behind a earthworks wait for the order to fire from their officer. Their machine gun is a 'war booty' Japanese Taisho 3 which was produced from 1914 and served with the Imperial Army until 1945. The Taisho 3 was the older of the two medium guns in service with the Imperial Army in the Second World War. Although the Nationalists did use captured Japanese small arms during the Civil War they were more likely to employ the heavier weaponry such as artillery and tanks.

A supply column of the Nationalist Army moves towards the front with boxes of ammunition strapped to the backs of the horses. Throughout the Civil War both sides still had to rely largely on horses or mules to move most of their supplies. Large numbers of Japanese trucks and other vehicles had been captured in August 1945 and the U.S. had supplied many others. The lack of servicing in most case meant however that only a fraction of the vehicles in the Army were serviceable at any one time. Large numbers of Japanese helmets were also captured at the end of the Second World War and the two soldiers in the foreground are wearing M32 models. Canadian made Sten sub-machine guns were also supplied in large numbers to the Nationalists and the man marching at the head of the column is armed with one.

Below: Soldiers of one of the elite 'fire brigades' of General Fu Tso-yi assemble at the town of Paoting, 120 miles north of Peking in February 1948. General Fu had a reputation as one of the more capable Nationalist commanders during the 1946-1949 fighting and had twenty-eight divisions with 280,000 men under his command. His men were also some of the best in the Nationalist Army and included about 100,000 'personal' troops who owed loyalty to him. The General was heavily depended on by Chiang Kai-shek to hold the North of China for the Nationalist Government. General Fu was a pragmatist however and when his forces holding Peking were surrounded he negotiated a peaceful handover to the Communists on the 20th of January 1949. Fu's men are well dressed in the new winter issue uniform of the Nationalist Army and are armed with a mixture of Springfield M1903 and P17 rifles.

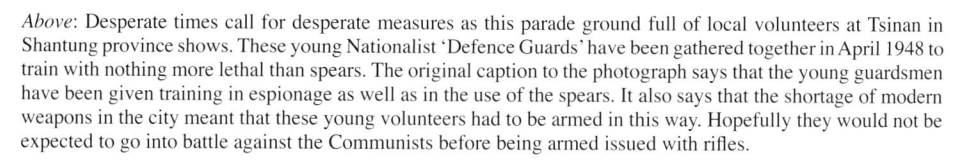

Above: Desperate times call for desperate measures as this parade ground full of local volunteers at Tsinan in Shantung province shows. These young Nationalist 'Defence Guards' have been gathered together in April 1948 to train with nothing more lethal than spears. The original caption to the photograph says that the young guardsmen have been given training in espionage as well as in the use of the spears. It also says that the shortage of modern weapons in the city meant that these young volunteers had to be armed in this way. Hopefully they would not be expected to go into battle against the Communists before being armed issued with rifles.

Below: Female Defence Guards from the city of Tsinan march past an army barracks to the parade ground dressed in newly issued uniforms in April 1948. The dark blue outfits worn by the girls have no insignia at all on them and may be surplus police uniforms and are worn with U.S. supplied 'baseball boots'. Unlike their male counterparts in the previous photograph they have not been issued with spears and would usually perform support and nursing roles.

Looking out over the barbed wire of a guard post in the Summer of 1948 this soldier is well armed with a Thompson M1A1 sub-machine gun. Unusually for this period the gun still has the old fashioned looking muzzle compensator fitted. The soldier carries his spare magazines for the Thompson in the belly pouch which has four pockets. His uniform is basically the same as the type worn by most Nationalist troops from 1937 until 1946. Because of the chaos of the war many Nationalist soldiers would have worn this uniform until the end of the war in 1949.

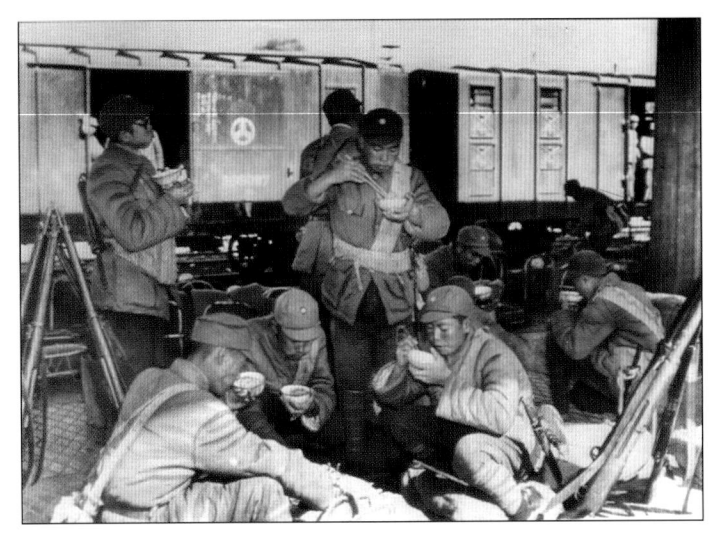

Soldiers of the White Sun

Nationalist troops have a quick meal in Pukow Railway station during a break from the fighting on the 16th of November 1948. They have just thrown back a Communist attack in the fighting around Suchow but even as they rest the enemy is regrouping for another offensive. The men have stacked their Japanese Arisaka 38 rifles where they can quickly reach them in an emergency.

In November 1948 soldiers forming the Nationalist garrison of Peking are setting up camp in the grounds of the ancient 'Temple of Heaven' within the Forbidden City. The men are part of General Fu Tso-yi's Army which was to surrender the city to the Communists a few months later without a fight. The photograph shows the dramatic changes that had taken place in China when only a few decades before the only people allowed into the Forbidden City under pain of death were the royal family and their entourage.

A total of thirty-six unarmed M5 light tanks are loaded onto a ship at Houston Texas for shipment to the Nationalist Government in Shanghai on the 18th of November 1948. Although the U.S. government did send some armoured vehicles to the Nationalists the amounts were never sufficient to turn the tables against the Communists. Other armour sent to the Nationalists included a shipload of U.S. M8 motor gun carriages armed with 75mm howitzers. A large number of armoured vehicles ordered by the Nationalists never got to China and U.S. Department of State records from 1949 show that 200 'used' light armoured cars were earmarked but never sent. The same records show that the British government was ready to send 200 Staghound armoured cars and eighty-five Sherman tanks to the Nationalists in 1949. These British war surplus vehicles were reported as being 'in transit' but were certainly never got to China before the Nationalist government fell.

This lone Nationalist sentry guards one of the improvised armoured trains used especially in Manchuria during the Civil War. The flat bed truck that he is guarding has been equipped with a protected guardhouse and a reinforced bunker with railway sleepers. To stop Communist insurgents for climbing on the truck it has been covered in barbed wire.

Civil War, 1946-1949

Above: A unit of seven U.S. supplied M5 light tanks prepare to move off to spearhead a Nationalist attack in the region of Suchow in 1948. Nationalist armour was usually employed in small units of a handful of tanks each during the civil war. Nationalist armoured units were never really able to exploit their numerical advantage over the Communists in the early part of the war. As more and more tanks fell into enemy hands any material advantage that the Nationalists had over the Communists was soon lost.

Left: The crew of a U.S. 105mm M101A1 howitzer fire their gun towards Communist lines during fighting in the Suchow region in 1948. During the Second World War the U.S. supplied the Nationalists with over 400 of these up to date field guns to China from 1943. Any that the Communists captured were gratefully received and were immediately put back into service against their previous owners.

A government armoured train steams out of a Manchurian city in an attempt to keep the communications between the Nationalist held enclaves open. For much of the civil war in Manchuria the various Nationalist garrisons were isolated by miles of Communist held countryside from each other. Although the strength of these garrisons meant that they could not be easily taken they seldom ventured outside the confines of their cities. There were few attempts by the Nationalists to retake territory held by the Communists in Manchuria. They were content to hold onto the cities and towns and the main lines of communication like the railway between them. The armoured rail car in the foreground has a number of firing ports along its side and on the front has a rotating turret armed with a Type 24 heavy machine gun.

165

Soldiers of the White Sun

Above: Stood on a siding in the railway station of a Manchurian city this Nationalist armoured rail car with the Nationalist insignia on the front is going to be coupled up to the train behind it. Even with the protection of the rail car, small trains like this would he have been easy for determined Communist guerrillas to attack. The Communists also used sympathetic locals to tear up the railway tracks in front and behind trains to immobilise them and make them easy targets.

Right: The Nationalist crew of an ex-Japanese Type 95 'Soki' tracked armoured railway vehicle in Manchuria are ready to board before going on a mission. Type 95s were basically tankettes which were fitted with retractable wheels so they could run on rails as well as on land. Although the Type 95 could be converted from running on rails to running on its tracks in 1 minute it is doubtful if the Nationalists used it for that purpose. They probably used it solely in its railway role to patrol ahead of vulnerable trains operating a supply network between Nationalist held positions.

This ex-Japanese Type 91 armoured railway car of the Nationalist Army is being prepared to go on patrol along the Manchurian railways. These armoured cars converted to run on the rails were used extensively by the Japanese during their occupation of Northern China. Those that fell into Nationalist hands in 1945 in working order were used by them in Manchuria. The Type 91 was armed with six machine guns mounted at the front, back and with several along its side with another in the rotating turret. Photographs show the use of large numbers of captured Chinese ZB-26 light machine guns by the Japanese.

Civil War, 1946-1949

In December 1948 as Communist forces advance towards Nanking a unit of Nationalist cavalry move up to the front. Even though there were mechanised units in both the Communist and Nationalist armies during the Civil War, Cavalry was vital to both sides during the conflict. Nanking was to hold out until April 1949 when the capital of Nationalist held China was then moved to Canton. The troopers at the front of the column are all armed with U.S. supplied M2 carbines which were supplied in large numbers to the better Nationalist units.

Chiang Kai-shek leaves the National Assembly in January 1949 to the acclaim of parading Nationalist troops. By this date the war was all but lost by the Nationalists and during the remainder of 1949 was to see repeated defeats at the hands of the Communists. Chiang plans to withdraw his regime to the island of Taiwan were already well advanced with some of the best units and equipment being shipped there by early-1949.

Two armoured cars guard the National Bank in Shanghai on the 25th of February 1949 as 3,000 desperate refugees from Communist controlled China try to withdraw their money. The bank was in fact protected by twelve of these armoured cars which were locally built in government workshops. Improvised on truck chassis the cars were armed with two Type 24 heavy machine guns, one in the front and one mounted in the turret. This type of armoured car was just one of several manufactured by the Nationalists during the Civil War. They were alright for this kind of crowd control but were not really heavily enough armoured for combat. Also protecting the bank is a unit of 'elite' police who wore a special black uniform with a M35 German steel helmet.

Soldiers of the White Sun

This photograph shows the view from behind the previous image of the National Bank of Shanghai in February 1949. The men guarding the bank are a mixture of regular troops in their grey padded uniforms and 'war booty' Japanese steel helmets and armed police. As mentioned in the previous caption the police are wearing old M35 steel helmets which were also still in service with some regular units.

A heavy machine gun crew take a break from firing their Browning M1917 while waiting for the next Communist attack. Nationalist soldiers were said by observers to perform much better in defence than in offensive situations. This hastily prepared position would not however be able to hold for long against any determined Communist assault.

During the build up to the defence of Shanghai in March 1949 a Nationalist Artillery officer takes a ride back to his unit with fodder for his draught horses. While the officer shelters from the rain his more unfortunate soldier leads the mule and gets soaking wet. This photograph sums up much that was wrong with the Nationalist Army by 1949 with indifferent officers leading demoralised soldiers who were all waiting for their inevitable defeat.

Above: On the 23rd of April 1949 Nationalist troops march to their positions in defence of Shanghai from the Communists. The men are described in the original French caption as carrying anti-tank guns which may be U.S. 75mm M20 recoilless rifles. By the 16th of May Shanghai was virtually surrounded by the Communist 3rd Field Army and the Nationalist commander General T'ang En-po vowed to turn the city into another 'Stalingrad'. When the final attacks were launched on the 25th of May the city fell easily to the Communists but not before most of the Nationalist troops had been evacuated to Taiwan.

Right: General Wang Yu-chi the officer in command of the defence of Chinkiang in April 1949 points out possible points of Communist attack to a sentry. The General is wearing the post 1946 officers uniform in khaki wool with the U.S. style peaked cap. Even this late in the Civil War the sentry wears a pre-1945 pattern ski cap with his padded winter uniform.

Soldiers of the White Sun

Above: This mass parade takes place at the headquarters of General Ma Hung-ku'ei in Ningsia Province in remote northwestern China on the 2nd of May 1949. Guest of honour at the parade was Major-General Claire Chennault the former commander of the famous 'Flying Tigers' AVG. General Ma was regarded as one of Chiang Kai-shek's more reliable commanders and held his remote province loyally for the Nationalists until his troops deserted him. The rotund Ma was known for his love of ice cream and always offered his guests large amounts of it. General Ma's troops here look like an army from the 19th Century with their horse drawn limbers for their 75mm field guns and PAK 35/36 anti-tank guns. When the Communists advanced on their province in September of this same year Ma's Army surrendered and he went into exile

Right: In early May 1949 an improvised armoured car of the Nationalist Army drives through the streets of Shanghai. This type of armoured car was built in large numbers in Chinese government workshops during the Civil War on a truck chassis. They were built in several models and were usually only armed with M24 machine guns in the turret and at the side of the drivers compartment. A few were produced with an improved main armament of a 20mm light cannon mounted in the turret.

Artillery of General T'ang En-po's Army moves through the centre of Shanghai to take up positions on the 17th of May 1949. The howitzer in the foreground is a 'war booty' Japanese 150mm Model 4 1915 which was utilised by the Nationalists as one of the main heavier artillery pieces during the Civil War. Both sides in the conflict were pleased to use any captured Japanese equipment and the Communists continued to use it for many years after their victory in 1949. Even though the Nationalists did receive some modern heavy artillery from the U.S. there were never enough to replace the older models.

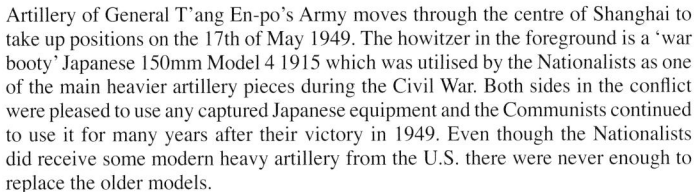

Medium artillery is moved up to the outskirts of Shanghai on the 17th of May 1949 as the final battle for the city begins. This unidentified 75mm field gun is probably a modified Japanese model captured by the Chinese in 1945. Although the Nationalist commanders in the city had promised to hold out and turn the city into a 'Second Stalingrad' the reality was different. The fighting only lasted for a few days later with the city falling on the 25th but not before most of the garrison had been evacuated to Nationalist sanctuary on Taiwan.

Nationalist Marines are transported in a Naval landing ship along the Chinese coastline to relieve a besieged position in 1949. The Chinese Marines Corps had been formed in December 1914 from the old Naval Sentry units. On the left sleeve of the man in the foreground is the cloth patch of the Marines which is similar in design to the U.S. Marine Corps badge. Most of the men are armed with bolt-action rifles while one marine at the back of the group is armed with a U.S. M3 grease gun sub-machine gun.

A young Nationalist Naval infantryman stands guard over a barracks in 1949 with his Mauser rifle slung over his shoulder. On the front of his archaic looking peaked cap is the metal enamelled badge of the Chinese Nationalist Navy. During the Civil War the Nationalist Navy performed a variety of tasks including transporting men and supplies. With no Communist Naval forces to contend with the Nationalist Navy should have had a more vital role in the Civil War. Its performance was affected however by low morale and a high level of corruption amongst its officers.

Soldiers of the White Sun

This photograph quite succinctly sums up the position of the two warring parties by 1948-1949. The prisoners of war are Nationalist troops who are being guarded by Communists wearing captured U.S. steel helmets. By the time this photograph was taken the Nationalists were losing the war and these men would have probably quite happily joined them. Many ordinary Chinese just wanted the fighting to end and had little to lose by a Communist victory.

Captured Nationalist troops in late-1949 are marched to an assembly point as the demobilisation of the huge number of defeated soldiers begins. Fighting continued until the end of 1949 and in some remote regions into the following year but the Nationalists were effectively defeated long before that. They were not helped by the large number of Nationalist commanders who defected taking their troops over to the Communists as defeat became inevitable.

This patriotic Nationalist poster from 1949 shows General Li Tsung-jen the victor of the Battle of Taierhchuang in 1938. He was one of the few loyal high-ranking officers of the Nationalist Army as the Civil War drew to its conclusion. His loyalty was to the Nationalist government as a whole rather than to the personal leadership of Chiang Kai-shek. He was elected against Chiang's wishes as Vice President by the Nationalist assembly in March 1948.

Chinese Army Uniforms, Equipment and Weaponry, 1931-1949

A smartly dressed soldier of the Nationalist Army guards a public building in Northern China in 1932. Although he is wearing the standard cotton uniform he is just a little better turned out than the average soldier. Ski caps were a recent introduction to the Chinese Army and most of his comrades would still be wearing the peaked cap. He carries his Hanyang Type 88 carbine slung casually over his shoulder, and his only equipment are his canvas ammunition bandoliers.

This crewman of an armoured train in Manchuria in 1931 is dressed in the same basic uniform as worn by the Nationalists during their campaigns of the late-1920s. He wears a large peaked cap and scruffy cotton tunic and trousers that were probably in a nondescript khaki colour. His menacing fighting sword is a crudely made weapon that was widely used by Chinese soldiers during the 1920s and early-1930s. As with many of these swordsmen he has also been issued with a Mauser C-96 broom handle pistol which was imported into China in large numbers.

173

Soldiers of the White Sun

Above: This heavily posed photograph from the 1932 fighting shows an officer and his men emerging from a dugout. The officer throwing the hand grenade is wearing a double-breasted padded winter coat over the top of his khaki woollen jacket and trousers. His two men have heavily wadded cotton overcoats on with one having a hood attached while the other does not appear to have one.

Right: In this tinted postcard from 1932 we see two types of winter clothing worn by the Chinese Army at that time. The officer on the right wears the double-breasted padded cotton overcoat in khaki cotton over the top of a grey cotton jacket and trousers. His comrade firing the light anti-aircraft gun wears wadded cotton jacket and trousers with puttees all in grey cotton.

Chinese Army Uniforms, Equipment and Weaponry, 1931-1949

Right: In this photograph taken in 1936 a group of Chinese officers on an exercise examine a military map. They all wear standard officers service dress as introduced in the early-1930s and worn by some until 1949. The collar rank bars can just be made out on the General in the foreground and have three gold three pointed stars on a gold background.

Below

Left: Two soldiers pose outside their barracks in 1936 wearing light khaki tunic and shorts with the American M1917 steel helmet. Their ammunition pouch belts look to be locally made and has four pouches on the chest and four on the waist belt. Footwear appears to be non-official issue gym shoes and both men have cloth leggings in different shades of khaki around the lower leg.

Right: This rear view of a Railway Guard at Tientsin station in 1936 gives a good view of the basic kit worn by many Chinese soldiers. He has a improvised blanket roll pack, a canvas bread bag and a metal water bottle in a canvas cover. Also strapped to his pack is a shovel which indicates that he is from a pioneer platoon. His arms are a mixture of the modern and the archaic with a Mauser rifle with bayonet fixed and on his back a fighting sword. The fighting sword is worn in a leather scabbard and has coloured tassels tied to the ring at the end of the hilt. So-called 'Big Sword' units were usually decimated by the Japanese before they get close enough to them to use the sword to good effect.

175

Soldiers of the White Sun

Above

Left: This immaculately turned out Major is pictured during a pre-war exercise directing the fire of machine gun crews. He wears typical officers service dress with his rank bar on his tunic collar and has the officers dress dagger on his belt. White gloves look a little out of place in the field even on peacetime manoeuvres and his outfit is completed by a pair of high officers riding boots.

Right: A soldier of the Northern Chinese Army which faced the brunt of the Japanese invasion in 1937 wears the peaked cap worn by many soldiers at that time. This model of peaked cap was not seen in use after 1937 when most of the units of the Northern Armies were destroyed by the Japanese offensive. He is armed with a German Maschinenpistole MP28/11 one of several types of German and Swiss produced sub-machine gun imported by the Chinese Army in the 1930s.

Left: A young soldier with camouflage netting over his shoulder and covering his field cap poses during the fighting in the autumn of 1937. He has a 'da-dao' fighting sword in its scabbard strapped to his back and is armed with a Hanyang Type 88 rifle. Any spare clips for the rifle are carried in the canvas bandoliers worn over his shoulder and across his chest.

Chinese Army Uniforms, Equipment and Weaponry, 1931-1949

Left: A Major of the 29th Army is pictured during the early fighting against the Japanese in the summer of 1937. His uniform is the basic khaki cotton officer's tunic worn with ski cap, and he has a brown leather Sam Brown belt. What makes this photograph interesting is the insignia carries on his chest and on one of his collar rank bars. The triangular cloth patch above his left breast pocket identification patch is non standard and has '29A' for 29th Army sewn on it. Also replacing the usual single three-pointed star on his rank collar is a small gold '29A' which also indicates the Army he serves in. Interestingly the wealth of this officer is indicated by the fact that he has a Parker fountain pen in his breast pocket.

Above: This cover photograph of an illustrated supplement of a 1937 pictorial magazine shows two soldiers 'preparing for the worst' by wearing gas masks against Japanese attacks. The rather strange appearance of the soldiers is added to by the wearing of camouflage foliage in their cotton peaked caps. Peaked caps of this type went out of service with the Nationalist soldiers after the defeat of the Northern Chinese Armies. The caption to the photograph says simply, 'Chinese soldiers equipped with anti-gas masks in the Pei-han front line'.

Left: This young soldier fighting in Shanghai in 1937 is wearing the standard light khaki uniform and has typical basic equipment. His locally made canvas bandoliers carry spare clips for his Mauser Kar.98k rifle as well as small items of kit. The canvas grenade bandolier has the usual two 'potato masher' Stielgranate 24 grenades secured in place with tapes around their wooden handle. Although large numbers of German made grenades were imported in the 1930s these were soon replaced by locally made copies which could be very crudely made.

177

Soldiers of the White Sun

These three photographs from a Chinese pictorial magazine of 1938 show the distribution of padded waistcoats to Nationalist troops in the winter of 1937-1938. The vests have been made by the Chinese Women's Association and are fitted on the soldiers by two of its younger members. Whenever possible Chinese soldiers were issued with a padded tunic and trousers as winter uniform but these garments would have certainly helped the soldiers keep warm.

The representatives of Chinese Women's Association distributing cotton-padded vests to Chinese defenders

Chinese Army Uniforms, Equipment and Weaponry, 1931-1949

This anti-aircraft gun crewman operating the battery rangefinder in 1938 is wearing standard uniform including the M35 steel helmet. On the collar of his tunic he has the special insignia of the anti-aircraft units with what appears to be a stylised brass listening device. The listening devices were used by anti-aircraft units to pick up the sound of planes overhead to pinpoint their position for the guns to aim at.

Above: During the confused fighting of the first year of the Sino-Japanese War this young soldier has been issued with a basic and improvised uniform. His headgear sums up the shortages suffered by the Nationalist Army as they lost so many men and so much equipment in 1937-1938. He has a raffia sun hat made to look from a distance like a British MKI steel helmet but of course offering little or no protection. The light khaki cotton shirt and shorts he wears were probably locally produced and he has not been issued with boots or even sandals. To complete his ad-hoc appearance his ammunition pouches for his FN-1930 short rifle also look locally produced.

Left: This patriotic cigarette card was produced by the Nanyang Brothers Tobacco Company of China in the 1930s. The inscription on the card translates as, "Return My Mountains & Rivers". In other words it extols the reader to help recapture the territory occupied by the Japanese since 1931. On the reverse of the card is text which demands that the Chinese work to stop their nations wealth being "drained into foreign hands". The bugler wears the grey cotton version of the Nationalist Army uniform and stands in front of a piece of heavy artillery.

179

Soldiers of the White Sun

'Generalissimo' Chiang Kai-shek appears at a 1939 rally wearing the model 1936 black full dress uniform of the Nationalist Army. His cap is a kepi style with the three gold rank bands of a General around the band and he also has the same bands around his jacket cuffs. The image is taken from a wartime propaganda magazine that extols the Chinese Army's resistance to the Japanese Imperial Army.

In this formal portrait of the late-1930s, Chiang Kai-shek poses in his full dress uniform without the kepi cap. The 1936 issue dress uniform harked back to the gaudy dress worn by the Chinese Warlords of the 1920s. Like many of the Warlords that Chiang had defeated in the late-1920s he has his chest festooned with awards presented to him by the 'grateful' Chinese nation.

Generalissimo Chiang Kai-shek poses for the camera in 1940 wearing standard officers woollen uniform. On his collar he wears the rank of Field-Marshal with a gold bar bordered in gold with three gold three pointed stars. Hanging from his brown leather Sam Brown belt is the Chinese Army dagger which was styled on similar ones worn by the Nazi Party in Germany. The influence of the German military advisors pervaded the Chinese Army in the mid to late-1930s.

Chinese Army Uniforms, Equipment and Weaponry, 1931-1949

This well turned out soldier on parade in 1942 is wearing a smart uniform and is equipped with everything that the Chinese Army could provide. His uniform is made from a good quality brown-khaki cotton and he has Lance-Corporals rank bars with three stars on his collar. He has a brown leather backpack, a canvas ammunition bandolier and a canvas bread bag over his shoulder. Most Nationalist soldiers apart from those few supplied by the U.S. would have been lucky to be a fully equipped as this man.

A young machine gunner from the Central Military Academy is on parade wearing his smart uniform made from a heavy gabardine khaki woollen material. The blue plastic discs on his collar indicate the name of his academy while his unit and personal details are carried on the patch above his left breast pocket. Not visible in this photograph is the white sun decal on the left side of his German imported M35 steel helmet. Slung over his shoulder is the standard ZB-26 light machine gun and this has its model and has its carrying strap fitted.

Soldiers of the White Sun

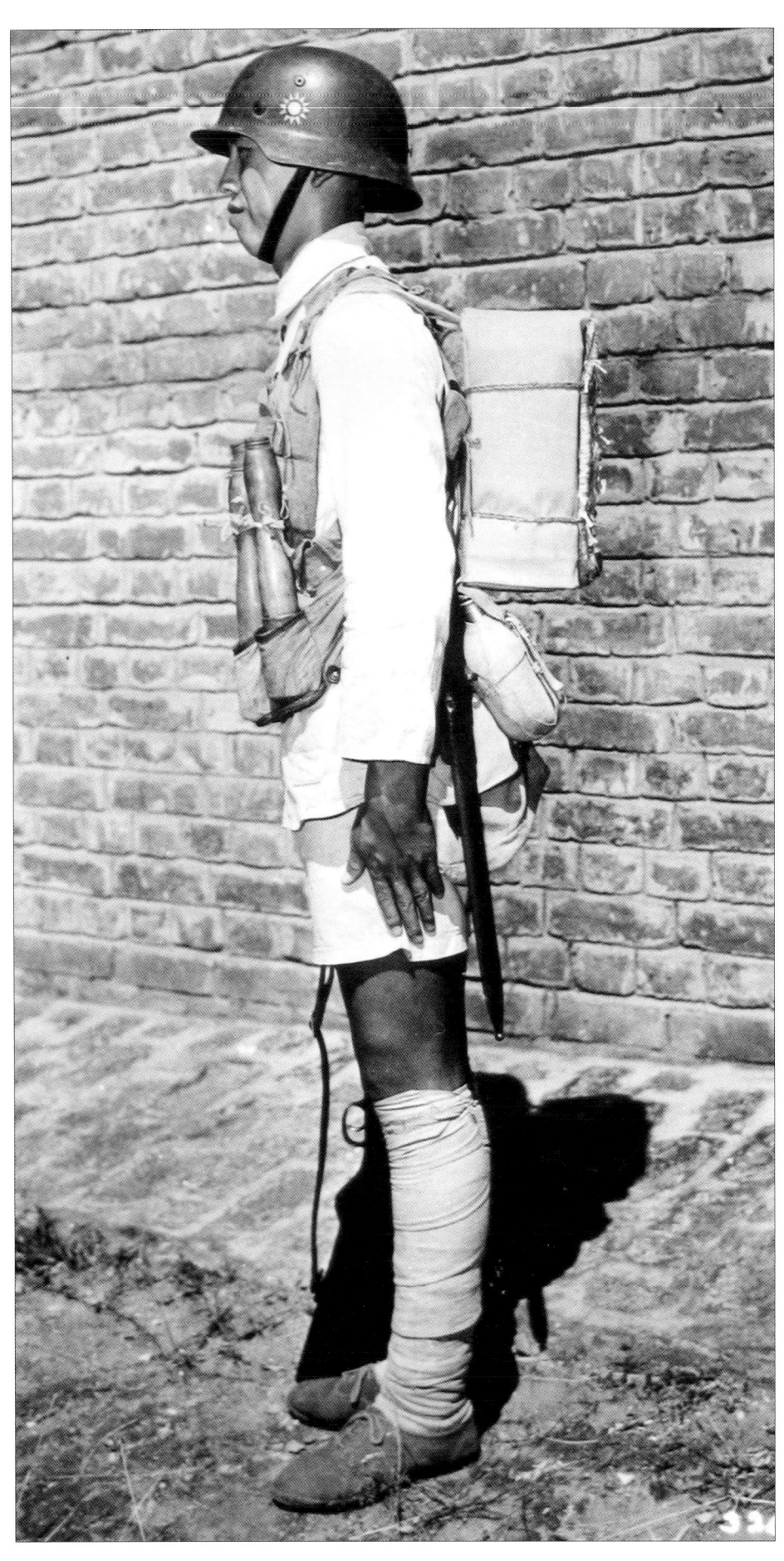

Left: This photograph and the next two images were taken by the U.S. Signal Corps in 1942 to record what uniform their 'new' allies the Chinese were supposed to have as regulation uniforms. In this side view we can see what would have been very rare full equipment with the grenade bandolier, water bottle and canvas bread bag. The backpack looks like it is made from a bamboo frame and he has a pair of straw sandals strapped to the back.

Opposite
The second U.S. Signal Corps photograph shows the front and rear view of the fully equipped Chinese Nationalist soldier of 1942. Both men wear scrupulously clean rough cotton shirts and shorts with ski caps made from the same material. Their roughly made brown leather shoes worn with cotton puttees would have been rather a luxury and some U.S. supplied X or Y Force troops still wore straw sandals. As well as the canvas grenade bandolier the man on the left has two ammunition bandoliers around his neck and waist. His comrade shows the rear view of his equipment with the backpack secured with home made rope.

Page 184
In the last Signal Corps photograph we have an officer and private modelling their uniforms complete with M35 steel helmets. The Captain had his rank bars on both collars and these have three 3 pointed stars running down the centre. His uniform is made from the same cotton cloth as the privates and is made up of a tunic with four pockets and a pair of cotton breeches. The puttees are made from a darker woollen cloth and are worn with black leather shoes in this case. Other higher-ranking officers would wear high boots with the breeches either in black or brown leather. Above the left breast pocket he has his name patch with all his unit details and his three Captains stars on the left.

Chinese Army Uniforms, Equipment and Weaponry, 1931-1949

183

Soldiers of the White Sun

Chinese Army Uniforms, Equipment and Weaponry, 1931-1949

Above

Left: This and the following two crude sketches were made by U.S. Intelligence Agents operating in China during the early-1940s. They were designed to show other agents what the 'friends and foes' fighting in China at the time would look like. This series also included coloured sketches of Japanese and Chinese puppet troops The caption to this sketch says simply 'Guerrilla' and this figure could represent either a Communist or Nationalist guerrilla fighter.

Center: This sketch shows a Nationalist soldier wearing the blue winter uniform which soon faded when worn to a blue grey colour. He is well armed and equipped with rifle, fighting sword and several stick grenades in his satchel.

Right: The Nationalist soldier in this sketch wears the light cotton khaki summer uniform worn from the early-1930s. This soldier's uniform is more olive green than khaki but basically any shade of brown and green were seen in use. He also has a straw sun hat on his back which came in various designs depending on the province that the soldier originated from or served in.

Right: This so-called 'surprise soldier' or commando is part of a platoon receiving training at the Pihu centre in Szechwan Province in 1943. His roughly made light khaki cotton tunic has his rank bar for Lance Corporal on the collar and he has his ID patch over his left breast pocket. Unusually for a Chinese soldier he is fully equipped with backpack, holdall and canvas bandolier and has a roughly made pick attached to the top of his pack.

185

Soldiers of the White Sun

Below

Left: Two smartly turned out Chinese sentries guarding the entrance to an air base in the early-1940s are relatively well uniformed and equipped. Although the photograph is not particularly clear you can see that they are dressed in light khaki cotton tunics, trousers and puttees and have captured Japanese M32 steel helmets on. On the front of the helmets they have the KMT sun emblem that appears to have been applied to stocks of captured helmets. They are both armed with U.S. made Thompson sub-machine guns, the left hand man having a M1 model while the other sentry has an earlier M1928AI model.

Right: These two sentries guarding a government building in 1944 are wearing a couple of rather unusual uniforms. The man on the left is wearing a green or brown khaki jacket and trousers with light khaki puttees. His hat appears to be a U.S. type service cap that was worn in large numbers after 1945 by the Nationalist Army but was not usually seen before that date. He has an armband on his left sleeve with Chinese characters which presumably indicates that he is a military policeman. His fellow sentry wears shirtsleeve order with his rank bar worn on the collar of his light khaki cotton shirt. The cap appears to be a U.S. Army side cap that suggests that they may be guarding an American airbase in China and have both been donated uniform items by their allies.

Above: Soldiers of the 185th Division in training with a Czechoslovakian ZB-26 light machine gun in the early-1940s. The crew both wear light khaki cotton summer uniforms with British MKI steel helmets with the Nationalist sun stencilled in white at the front. The 185D arm badge has black lettering on a white oval with a black background and edged in white.

Chinese Army Uniforms, Equipment and Weaponry, 1931-1949

In a photograph dated the 22nd of March 1944 a happy Chinese soldier of one of the U.S. trained Divisions has just successfully crossed the Tanai River in the Hukawng Valley in Northern Burma. The soldier is wearing Indian made KD overalls with a single breast pocket and zip up front over a British tropical aertex shirt. KD overalls were designed by the British Army to be worn by motorised and armoured troops as well as for general duties. His equipment is British webbing and he has pouches to carry spare magazines for his Thompson sub-machine gun. Helmets worn by the 'X' and 'Y' forces were either U.S. M2s or as in this case British MKI's.

Above: In September 1944 two soldiers greet each other on the Burma Front and illustrate the stark difference between U.S. supplied Chinese troops and the rest of the Nationalist Army. The soldier on the right belongs to a unit of the Chinese Army trained in India and is well clothed in khaki drill shirt, trousers leather boots and a U.S. M2 steel helmet. His comrade from the less well-supplied Yunnan based army does at least have a new cap with cloth sun badge on the front. The rest of his uniform however is standard Chinese issue cotton uniforms worn with a pair of homemade straw sandals. Also noticeable are the different physiques of the two soldiers with the man on the right having been well fed on full U.S. rations while his comrade has had to make do with smaller rations. When it comes to armaments the U.S. supplied soldier has been lucky enough to be issued with Thompson sub-machine gun. Although not fully visible here the Yunnan trained soldier is probably armed with a Belgian made FN1930 short rifle.

Left: Although this photograph is not particularly clear we can see that this soldier pictured in 1944 is from the Armies of southwestern China. He is well equipped with backpack and U.S. M1923 issue canvas belt with ammunition pouches. His rather scruffy jacket appears to be padded while his trousers are made from ordinary thinner cotton. The Adrian pattern steel helmet which he is wearing at an angle has a larger enamel or plastic sun emblem on the front.

Soldiers of the White Sun

These four pages are from the recognition booklet issued to U.S. soldiers in 1944 to help them identify their Allies uniforms and insignia. The pages show the collar ranks of the army and the cuff ranks of the Chinese Nationalist Air Force. Typical service dress of a Captain of the Air Force and a 2nd Lieutenant of the Army are illustrated.

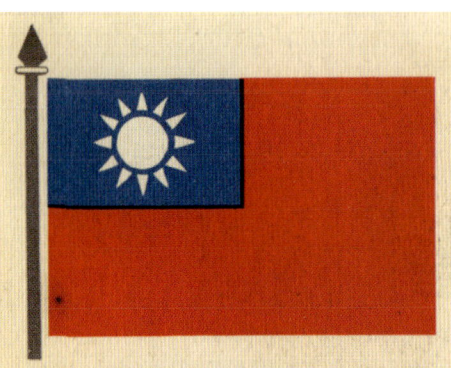

CHINA

★ Outdoors, the Chinese soldier salutes by hand but inside he executes a slight bow from attention. A junior of any rank salutes his seniors and addresses them not by rank but by the job assigned, such as "Company Commander" or "Section Leader." The Chinese soldier sometimes wears a removable band around his left arm to denote his outfit, and he proudly stands at attention when he hears the phrase "Long live Generalissimo!"

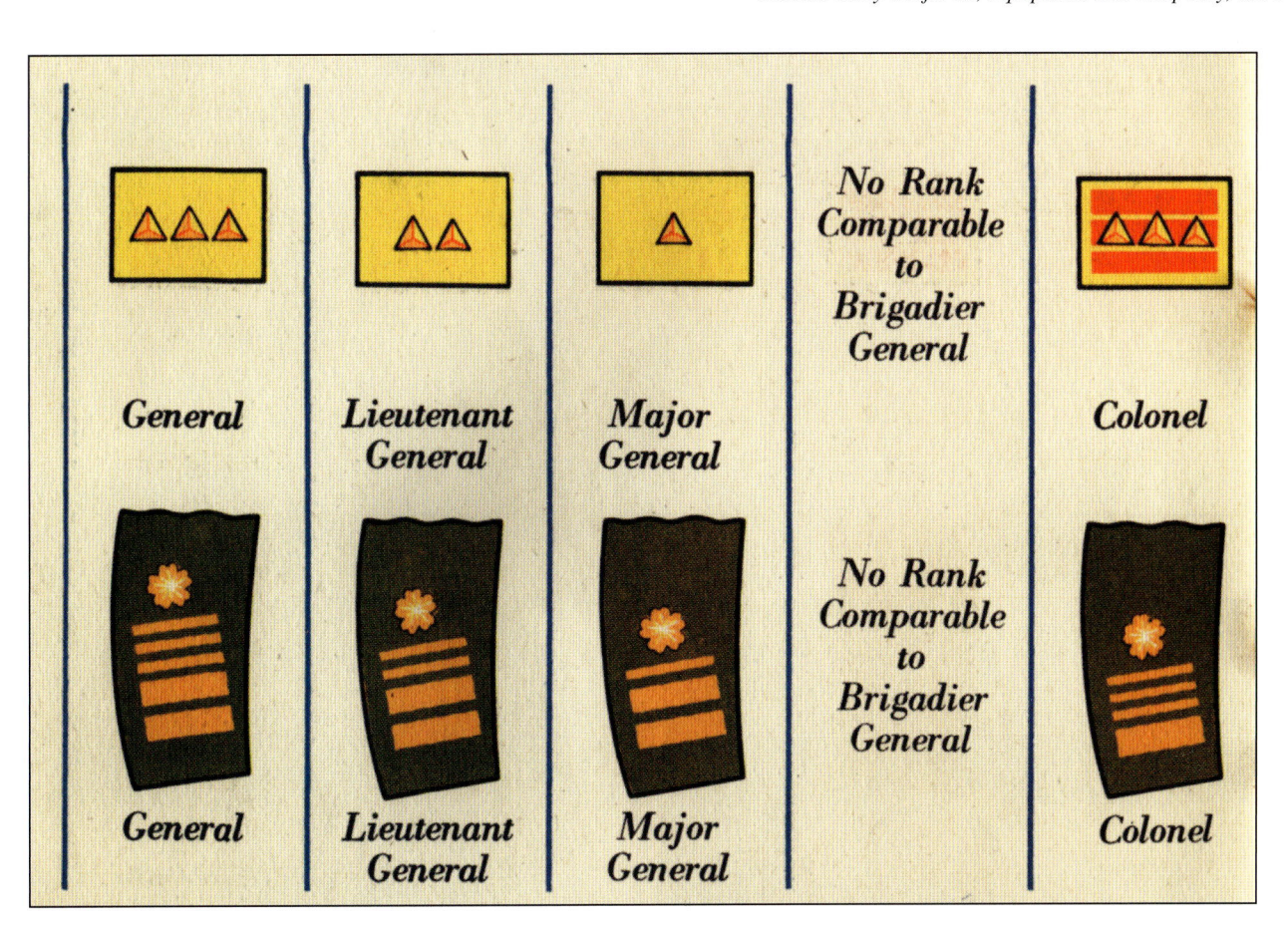

Chinese Army Uniforms, Equipment and Weaponry, 1931-1949

General	Lieutenant General	Major General	No Rank Comparable to Brigadier General	Colonel
General	Lieutenant General	Major General	No Rank Comparable to Brigadier General	Colonel

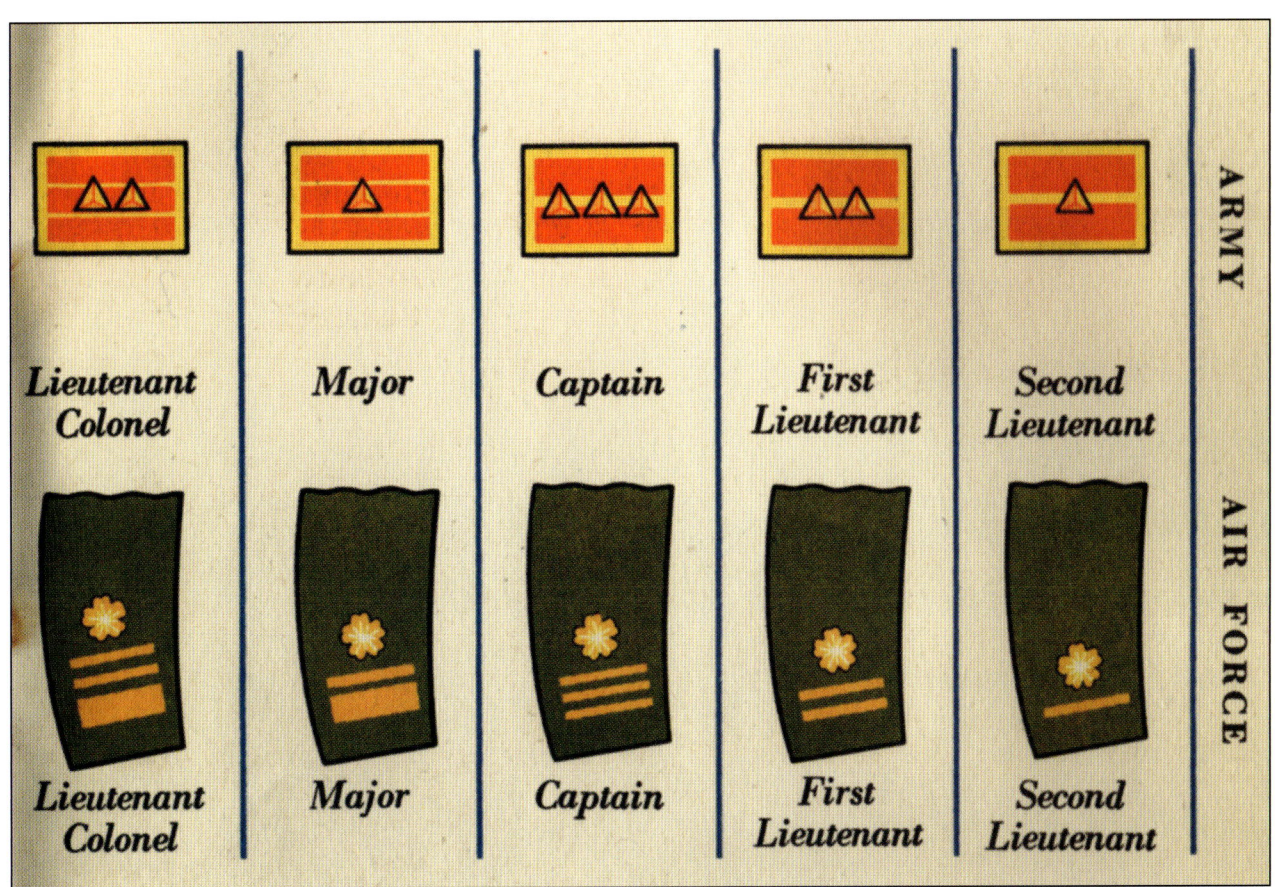 Lieutenant Colonel	Major	Captain	First Lieutenant	Second Lieutenant
Lieutenant Colonel	Major	Captain	First Lieutenant	Second Lieutenant

ARMY

AIR FORCE

Soldiers of the White Sun

Above: At the end of the war in 1945 this Nationalist sentry guarding a government building is equipped and armed from stocks of the defeated Japanese. His shirt and shorts are made from simple rough cotton and his field cap is again made out of the coarsest type of cotton. The soldier's pack and belt are captured Japanese issue made from brown leather and he is armed with a 'war booty' Arisaka 38 rifle with bayonet fixed. Japanese uniforms and equipment were utilised at the end of war by both the Nationalist and Communist Armies.

Below: In a close up from a previous photograph this guard of a government building in 1945 is wearing the smartest version of the pre-1946 uniform. He has a brown cotton cap, tunic and breeches with lighter coloured puttees worn with what appear to be Japanese brown leather boots. On his left upper sleeve he has a triangular patch that probably shows that he is from a headquarters guard. His canvas ammunition bandoliers appear to be empty with no spare clips for his 'war booty' Japanese Arisaka 38 rifle.

Opposite: A smartly dressed military policeman finds time to read a book before going out on patrol with U.S. Marines in late-1945. On the collar of his khaki wool uniform he wears his rank bars for his rank of 'Chung-Shih' or Sergeant. His Mauser C-96 automatic pistol is worn on his right hip and he has the brown leather cartridge belt that holds spare clips. Although only visible under magnification his brass buttons have the Nationalist sun design in their centre.

190

Chinese Army Uniforms, Equipment and Weaponry, 1931-1949

Soldiers of the White Sun

Chinese Army Uniforms, Equipment and Weaponry, 1931-1949

Opposite: A well-equipped and uniformed Nationalist soldier inspects the damage done to a factory recently vacated by the occupying Soviet Army in Manchuria in 1946. The Soviet Army either removed or destroyed most of the industrial capacity of Manchuria during their time there. The soldier wears a 'war booty' Japanese Imperial Army double-breasted wadded khaki cotton winter coat with a fur hat that could also be a captured item. As the Civil War went on the Nationalists produced their own issue winter fur hats with or without peaks.

Above: A twelve-year-old Nationalist boy soldier stands guard over his fellow soldiers kit as they are transported by sea to the Manchurian battlefields in 1946. The boy wears the same cotton uniform as his adult comrades with a couple of canvas bread bags to carry his personal gear in and a webbing snake belt. Over the top of his cotton ski cap he wears an ex-Japanese fur lined winter hat with the old Imperial Army yellow star badge still on it. He is armed with a Mauser short rifle which is just right for his size with its bayonet fixed but still in its scabbard.

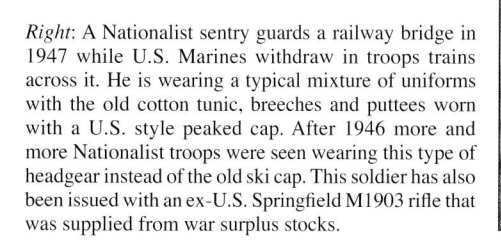

Right: A Nationalist sentry guards a railway bridge in 1947 while U.S. Marines withdraw in troops trains across it. He is wearing a typical mixture of uniforms with the old cotton tunic, breeches and puttees worn with a U.S. style peaked cap. After 1946 more and more Nationalist troops were seen wearing this type of headgear instead of the old ski cap. This soldier has also been issued with an ex-U.S. Springfield M1903 rifle that was supplied from war surplus stocks.

Soldiers of the White Sun

Left: This militiaman pictured in 1947 is a member of the Peace Preservation Corps which was one of the Para-military branches of the Nationalist army during the Civil War period. These men who were recruited locally to guard against Communist guerrillas were the poorest trained and equipped parts of the Nationalist military. This man only has his KMT cap badge to distinguish him from the Communist guerrillas and is armed with an ex-Russian Mosin-Nagant M1891 rifle. Peace Preservation Corps were regarded by the Communists as a good source of weaponry and by the regular Nationalist Army as second line troops. Their Nationalist comrades realised that PPC units were only brought into formations to make up the numbers.

Chinese Army Uniforms, Equipment and Weaponry, 1931-1949

Left Hand Figure: An infantryman in typical grey cotton uniform worn by the Chinese Army from 1931 until 1945. He has two canvas bandoliers each carrying 100 bullets and a canvas carrier for his German style stick grenades. The soldier's divisional patch on the left sleeve of his tunic would have his unit's Roman numerals in black in its center with for example '87D' for 87th Division.
Centre Figure: This officer wears standard officers service uniform from the 1937-1945 period which was made in various cloths although usually in wool. The uniform came in various shades of khaki but a brown shade was the most common colour. From his Sam Brown leather belt hangs an officer's dagger known as the 'spirit of the soldier'. Presumably the use of parade daggers came from the German military advisors whose army wore them in various patterns.
Right Hand Figure: This officer from the 1932 period wears a grey cotton tunic, field cap and breeches worn with black officers high boots.

Left Hand Figure: A typical Chinese soldier from the fighting in Northern China from 1932 until the outbreak of the Sino-Japanese War in 1937. He wears the British MKI steel helmet with a green-khaki tunic and breeches and puttees and has canvas bandoliers to carry ammunition for his Hanyang rifle.
Centre Figure: Another version of the uniform worn during the fighting against Japan in Northern China 1932-1937 is shown here. The soldier wears the British steel helmet and a grey cotton winter version of B1s uniform with an improvised pack made from a rolled blanket.
Right Hand Figure: This officer is a Lieutenant of the anti-gas troops in Northern China in 1937 and wears the British helmet with a smart officers khaki brown version of the standard uniform. Unusually he has button up canvas gaiters and wears the Chinese government-issue gas mask. On his left sleeve he wears a recognition armband which has stencilled on in red characters 'Chemical Troop'.

195

Soldiers of the White Sun

Left and Centre Figures: These two soldiers are wearing the uniform worn by the German trained Divisions of the Nationalist Army. Both men wear German produced M-35 steel helmets with their khaki woollen uniforms and have the full kit worn by a small majority of Chinese soldiers. Insignia on their uniforms is made up of a ID patch above the left breast pocket, a Divisional patch on the left sleeve and their rank bars on their tunic collars.

Right Hand Figure: This officer of the German trained Divisions wears the smartened up officers version of the other ranks uniform. Although of the same design as the uniform worn by the junior ranks it is just of superior manufacture. He is armed with a Mauser C-96 broom handle pistol and has an ammunition belt around his waist. The pistol is hanging from his Sam Brown belt in an holster formed by the hollowed out stock of the C-96.

Left Hand Figure: This soldier is from the Provincial forces fighting against the Inner-Mongolian 'puppet' army in Suiyuan province in 1936. He wears a fur hat and a fur lined coat over the top of his grey padded cotton tunic and trousers. His Thompson M1921 sub-machine gun may well have been produced in one the local arsenals in North-West China.

Centre Figure: This soldier is a mortar crewman from the 29th Army on field manoeuvres in the winter of 1936-1937. A few months later in July 1937, the 29th Army bore the brunt of the Japanese invasion of China. He wears padded grey cotton uniform including a cap which was particular to the 29th Army. His 'da-dao' fighting sword would probably be supplemented in battle with a Mauser C-96 or other pistol.

Right Hand Figure: A standard bearer from one of the Independent Brigades facing the Japanese invasion in July 1937 carries his units flag furled. His uniform is the grey cotton version of the standard light khaki summer uniform and he wears the German M-35 steel helmet. He is armed with a Mauser C-96 pistol which is worn on his right hip in a leather holster and he has ammunition pouches on his waist belt.

Chinese Army Uniforms, Equipment and Weaponry, 1931-1949

Left Hand Figure: This figure is a Lieutenant tank commander wearing standard tunic with a German padded leather crash helmet. He is armed with a C-96 automatic pistol presumably for protection when out of his armoured vehicle.
Centre Figure: A crewman of an Italian supplied CV-33 light tank wears Italian overalls with a padded crash helmet. The uniform presumably came with the light tanks when they were delivered from Italy in the mid-1930s.
Right Hand Figure: This Military Policeman wears an early pattern steel helmet and has an armband which carries the Chinese characters for 'MP'

Left Hand Figure: Private wearing the Summer uniform worn by most Chinese soldiers in the last few years of the Second World War. As well as light khaki cotton cap, shirt, breeches and puttees he has a raffia sun hat with patriotic messages painted on it.
Centre Figure: Another version of the latter war Summer uniform sees the soldier wearing loose fitting shorts with straw sandals. The sandals were often made by the soldiers themselves from materials supplied by their commanders.
Right Hand Figure: A trainee of the U.S. trained 'Y' Force wears British supplied Khaki Drill shirt and shorts with his Chinese supplied field cap.

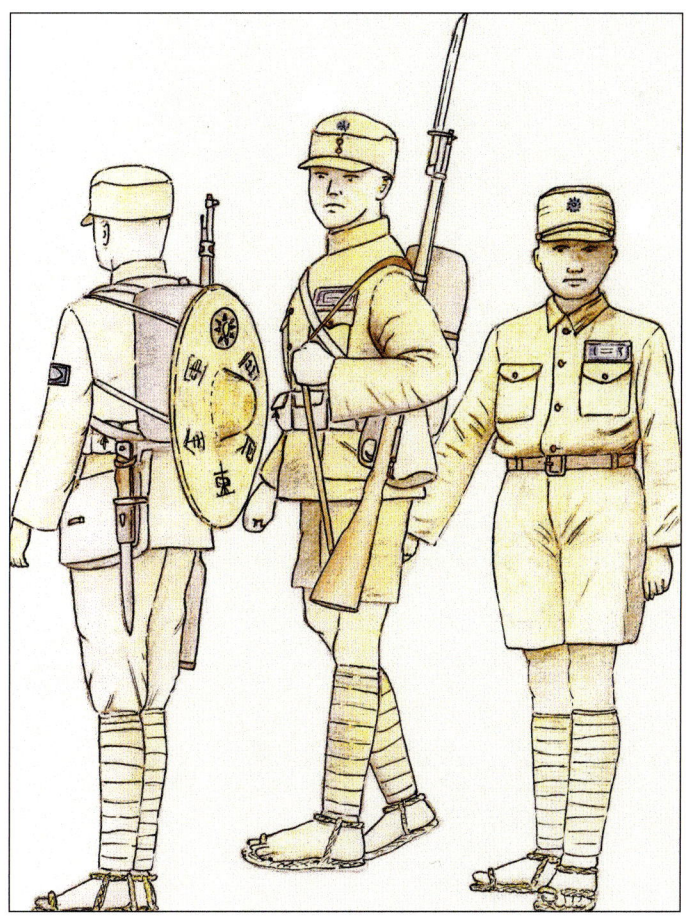

Soldiers of the White Sun

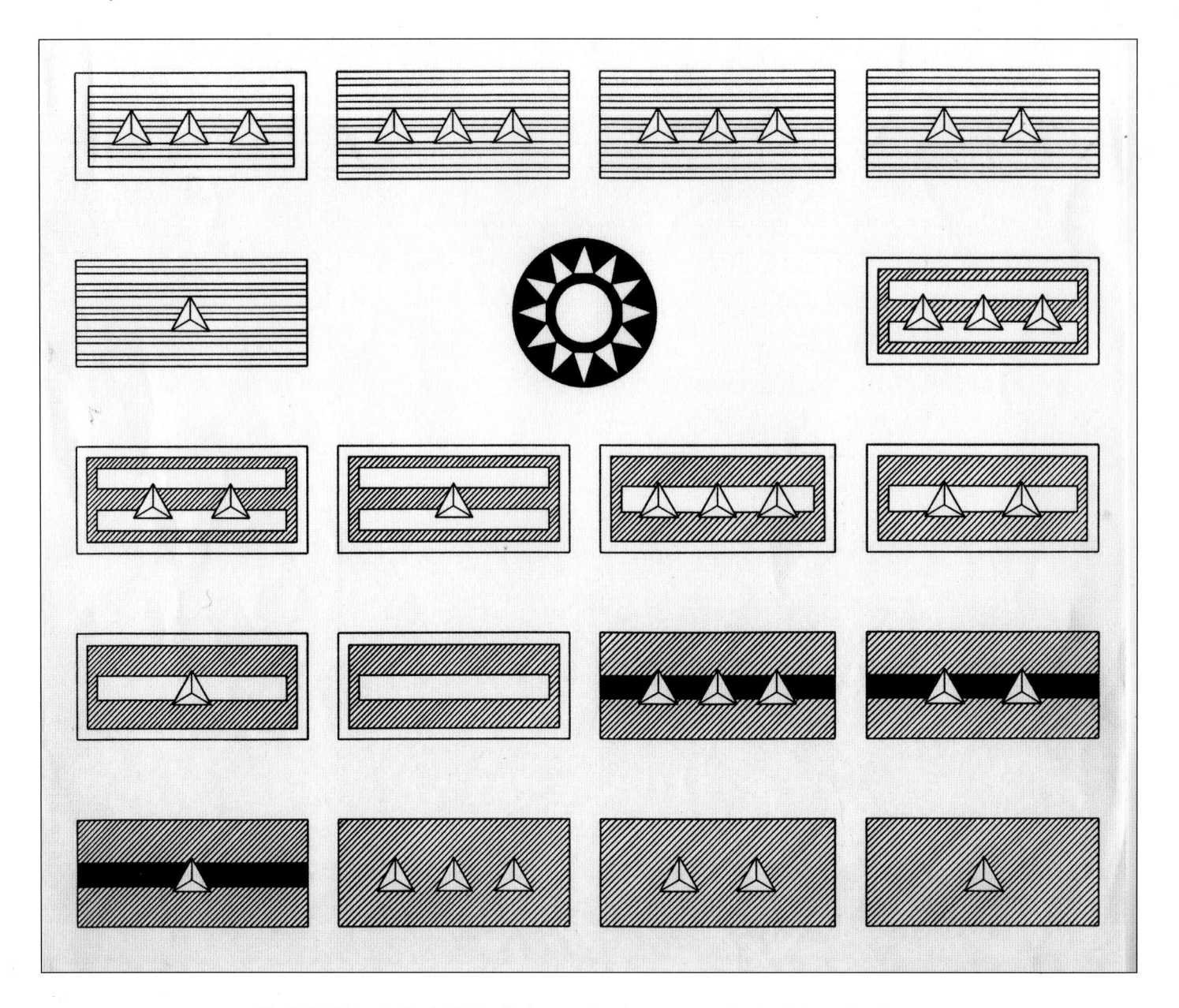

The 1929-1946 ranks for the Nationalist Army are based on a system using 1 to 3 three pointed stars on various backgrounds. They are from bottom to top and right to left: Bottom Row - Private, Private 1st Class, Lance Corporal, Corporal. Second From Bottom Row - Sergeant, Colour Sergeant, Warrant Officer, 2nd Lieutenant. Third From Bottom Row - Lieutenant, Captain, Major, Lieutenant-Colonel. Second From Top Row - Colonel, Major-General with Nationalist Army Insignia in the middle. Top Row - Lieutenant-General, General, Senior General, Field Marshal. The lowest three ranks from Private - Lance Corporal are on patches in the branch colour while the next three ranks from Corporal to Colour Sergeant have a black stripe through the centre. Ranks from Warrant Officer - Captain have one gold bar on a branch colour background and the next three ranks, Major - Colonel have two gold bars on a branch colour background. All General's ranks are on a gold background with the senior rank Field Marshal having a border around the edge. Branch colors were: gold – general staff, infantry – red, cavalry – yellow, artillery – blue, engineers – white, commissariat – dark red, medical – green, supply train – black, military police – pink.

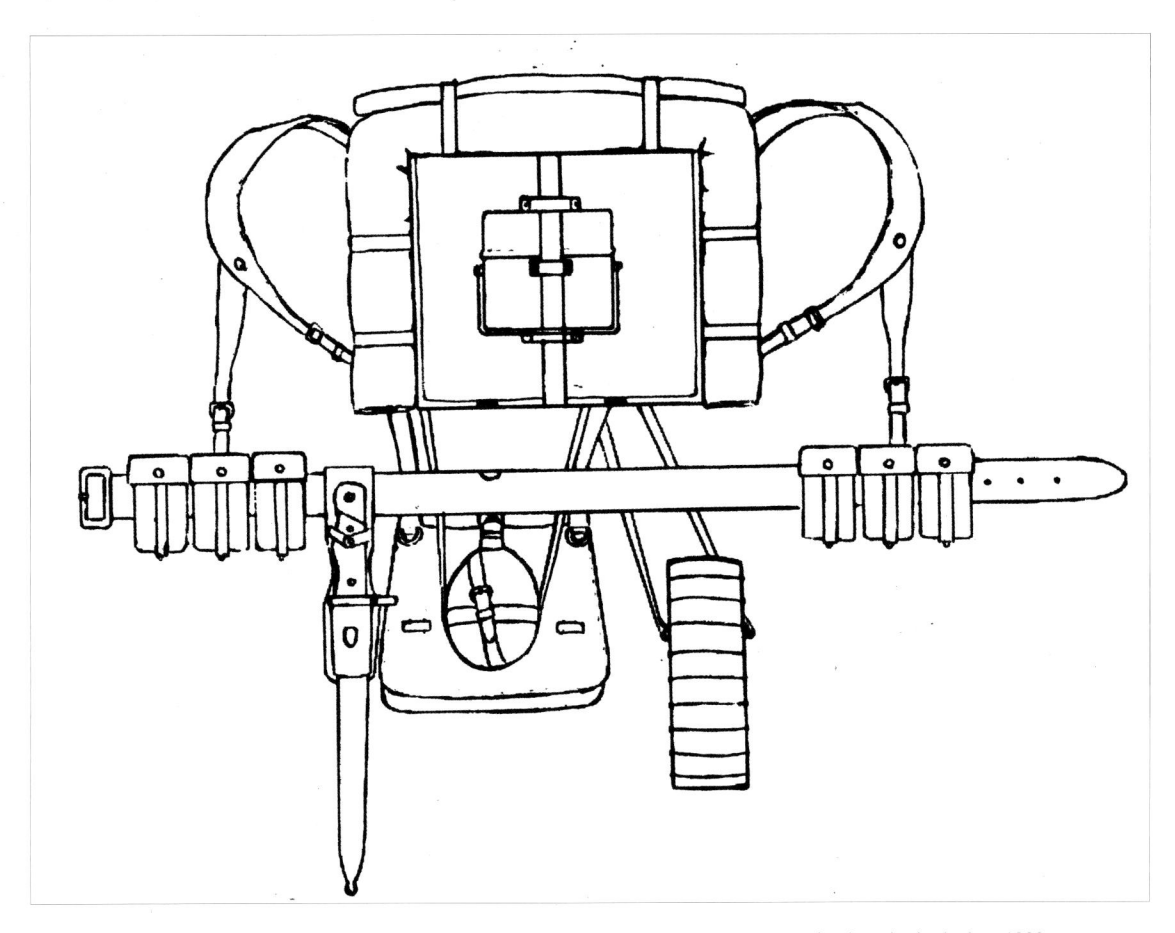

Chinese Army Uniforms, Equipment and Weaponry, 1931-1949

This is the ideal Nationalist soldiers equipment as issued to some of the German trained armies in the late-1930s. It consists of haversack, bread bag, tin canteen and water bottle with leather belts holding the Chinese version of the German ammunition pouches. A tin can holds the Chinese manufactured gas mask and hanging from the belt is the scabbard for the bayonet of whichever rifle the soldier has been issued.

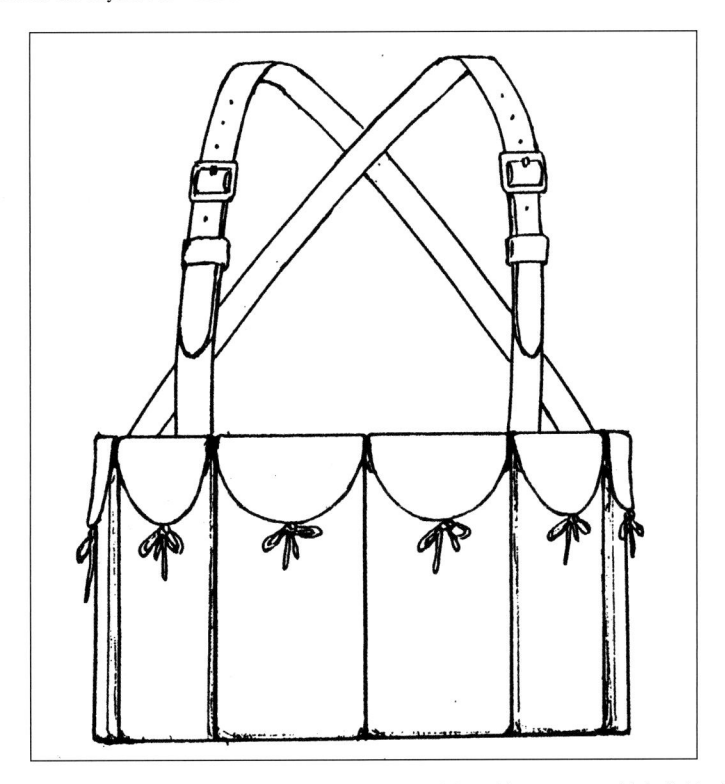

This canvas magazine carrier with leather straps was used by ZB-26 machine gunners with individual pouches for the guns magazines. When there was a two-man machine gun team the loader would wear the carrier while the other man carried the machine gun.

Soldiers of the White Sun

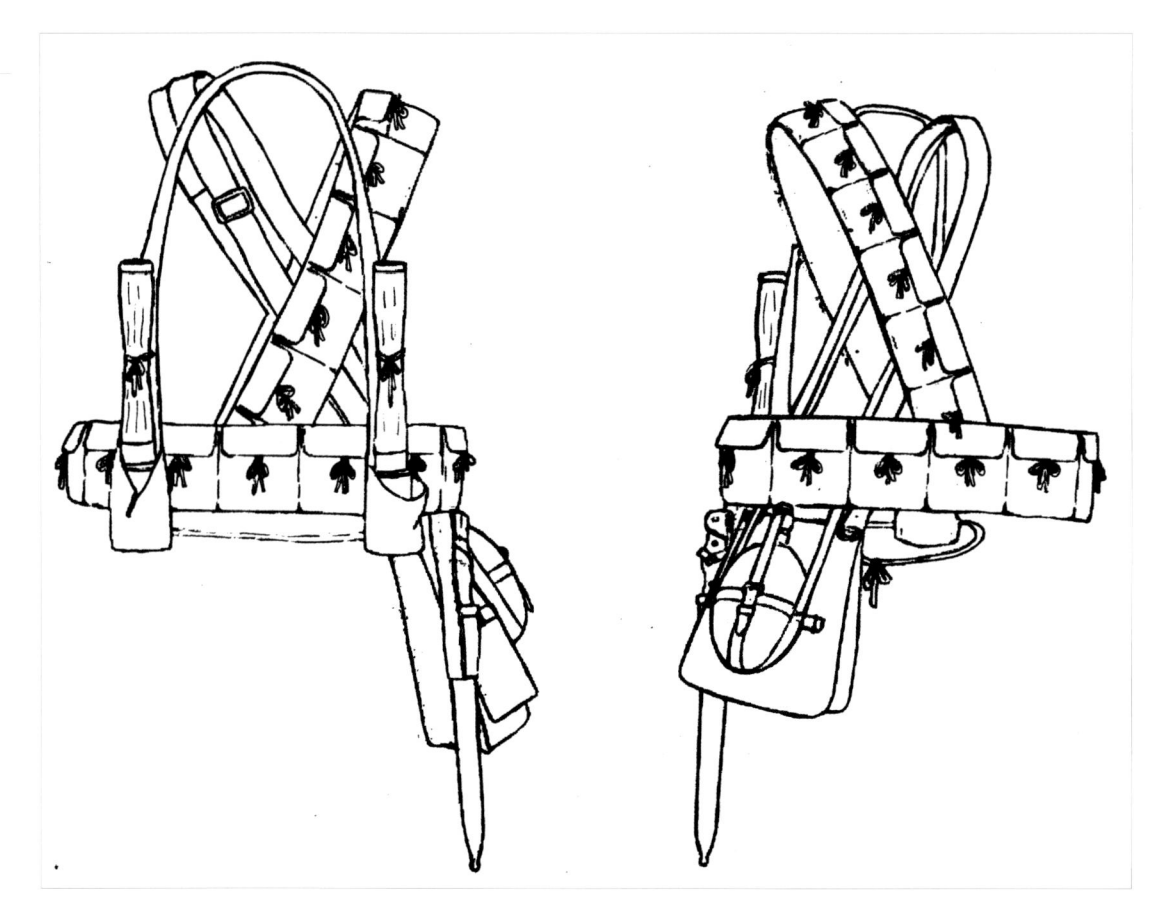

This is the typical equipment used by the vast majority of Chinese soldiers during the 1931-1945 period. In fact any soldier issued with this level of equipment would have considered himself extremely fortunate. It consists of two locally made canvas bandoliers carrying spare ammunition clips and a canvas holdall. The grenade carrier came in various designs but this version holds one 'potato masher' grenade on each side of the wearer's chest. Water bottles came in various models and were certainly not universally issued to Nationalist soldiers.

Chinese produced gas mask as issued to German trained Divisions of the Nationalist Army. The very real danger of Japanese gas attack meant that unlike in Western armies' masks were sometimes needed.

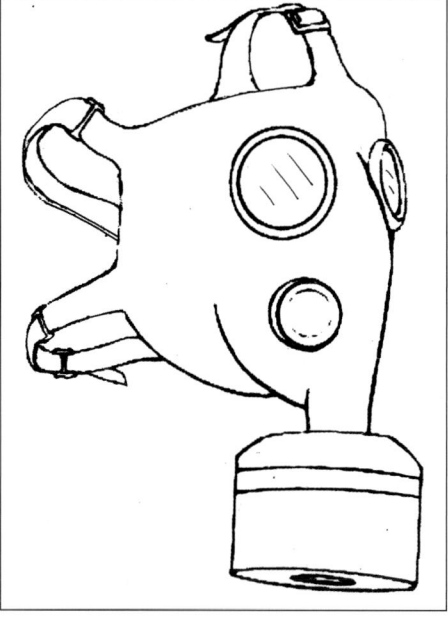

This model of gas mask was issued to some Provincial units of the Nationalist Army and may have been purchased by individual commanders for their troops. Many different models of gas mask were used by the Chinese and were imported from all over the world in the 1930s.

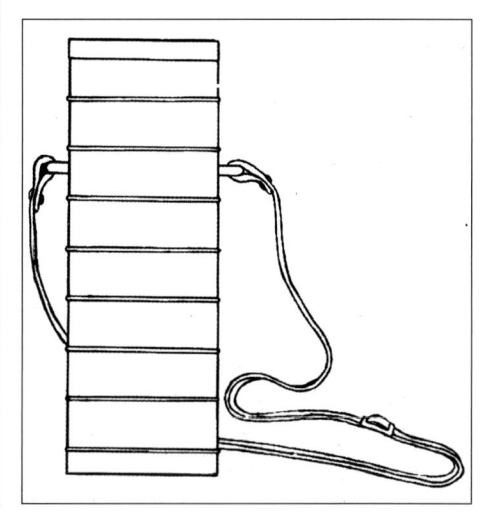

The tin canister with lid carried the standard issue gas mask but would have been issued to only the select units of the German trained Divisions of the army. There is very little photographic evidence of the canister being carried in battle and they may soon have been discarded or used for other purposes.

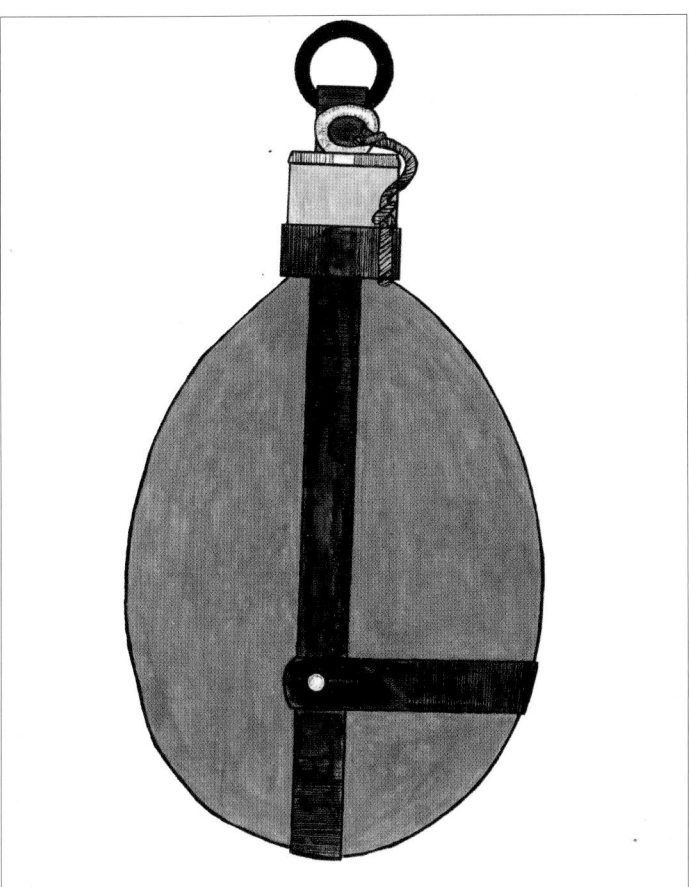

Chinese Army Uniforms, Equipment and Weaponry, 1931-1949

Left: This is an early 1st model of water bottle used by some Chinese units before 1937 and which fastened to the waist belt with a metal clip.

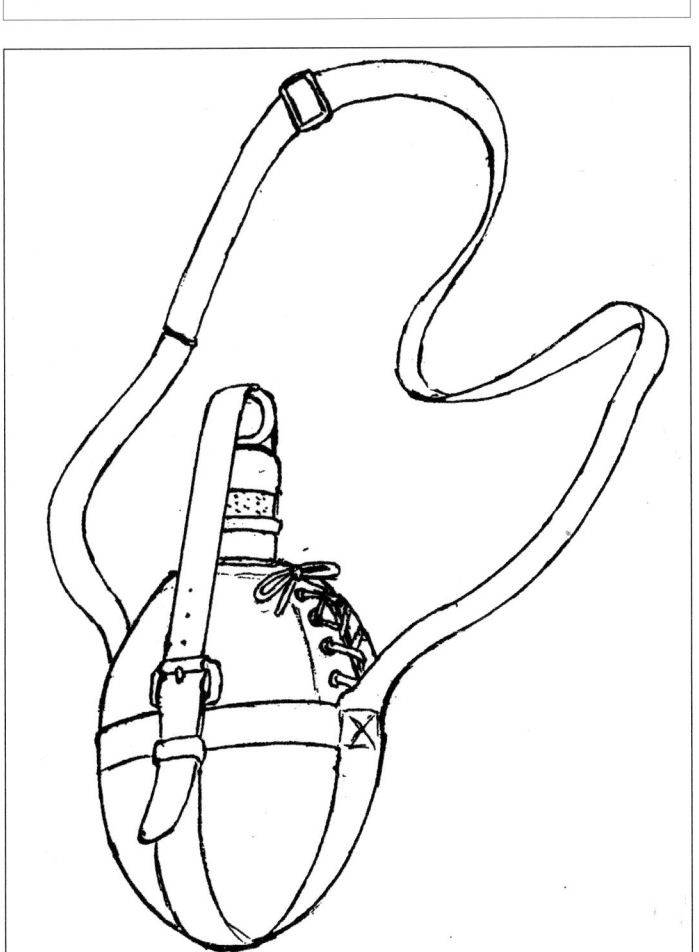

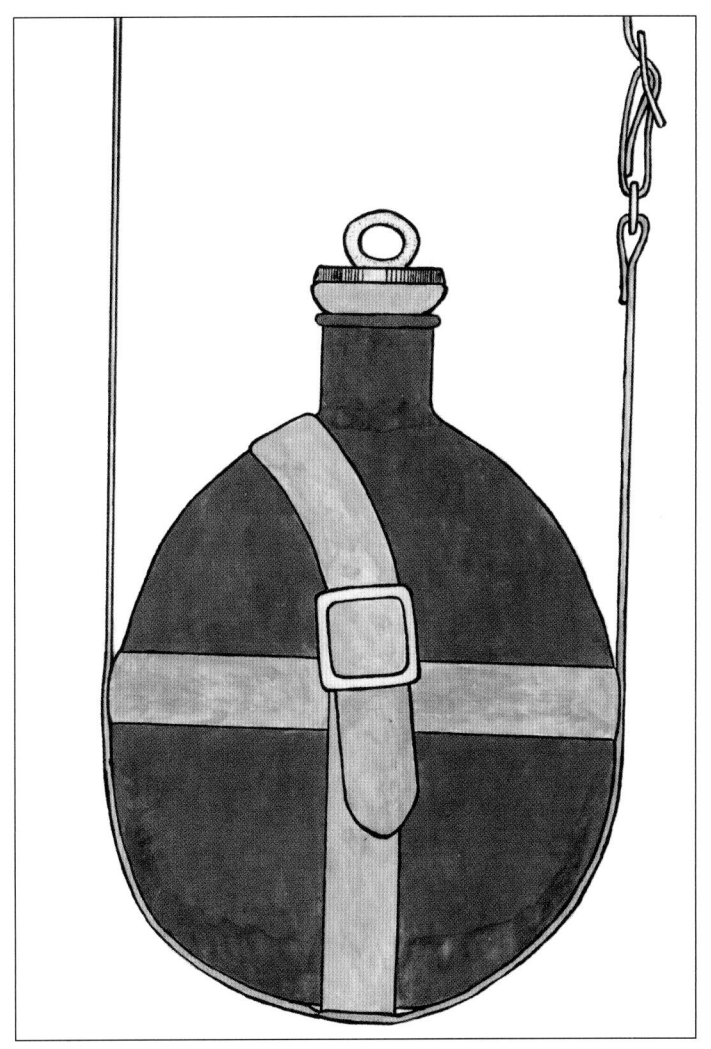

Above and left: Both illustrations show 2nd model of water bottle used by the German trained Divisions of the Nationalist Army. The bottle was covered with a green khaki cover and was carried with a brown leather strap over the shoulder.

Soldiers of the White Sun

Left: This in 1937 soldier is wearing a captured Type 95 Japanese gas mask for the news cameraman. Captured items like this would have been readily utilised by the Chinese Army which was always short of equipment.

Below: This illustration by Eric McChesney shows the officer's pattern dagger both in and out of its decorated scabbard. The dagger was worn by Nationalist officers with the service dress when on parade, but was probably on issue to some units. Like the German military and political daggers it was modelled on, it was never intended as a combat weapon.

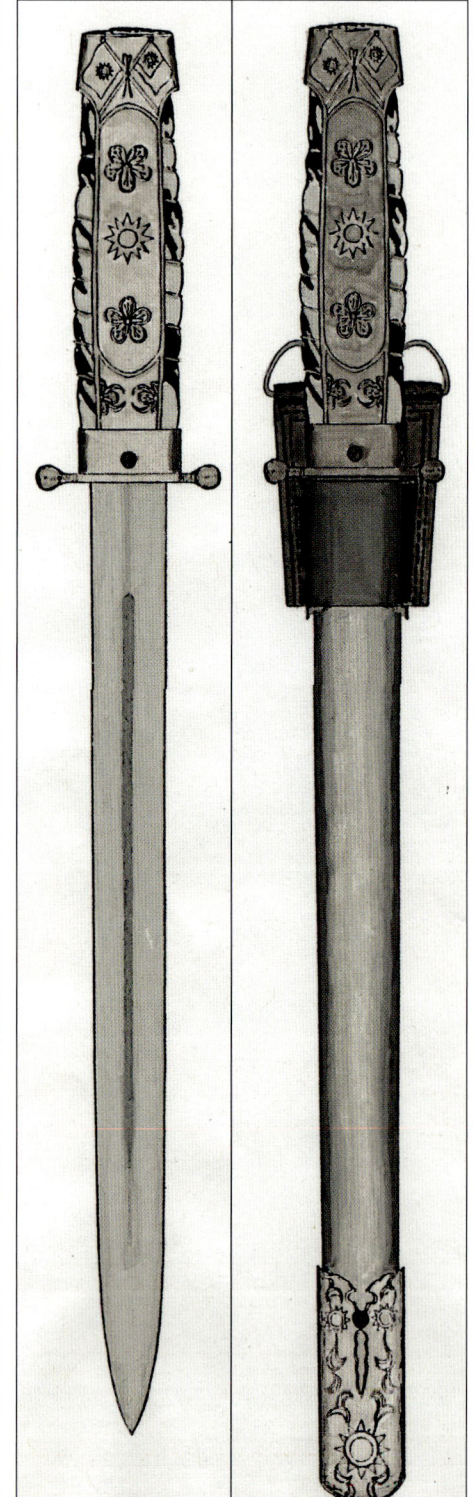

Along with the 'Chiang Kai Shek' rifle which was a copy of the Mauser Kar.98k, the 'Hanyang' Type 88 7.92mm Rifle was one of the most common rifles in Chinese service from 1931 to 1945. The Hanyang was modelled on the German Gew 88 with slight modifications and was manufactured in large quantities in several Chinese arsenals.

This Belgian made FN-1930 7.92mm short rifle was just one of several foreign produced Mauser rifles in service with the Chinese. China imported about 24,000 Belgian made FN rifles between 1930 and 1934 and these were a mixture of FN-24 standard rifles and FN-30 short rifles. Between 1937 and 1939 the Chinese bought a further 165,000 FN-30 rifles from Fabrique Nationale.

Soldiers of the White Sun

Czechoslovakia was a major source of armaments for the Nationalist Chinese with the VZ-24 7.92mm Short Rifle being the main rifle imported. In 1937 China purchased 100,000 VZ-24's which was suitable for the slight oriental frame of the average Chinese soldier.

This Type 21 Mauser 7.92mm short rifle was a Chinese produced copy of the FN-1930 and was produced at the Guangdong Arsenal in Kwangtung Province from 1932 to 1937. Like a lot of Chinese produced copies the manufacture of the Type 21 was not quite up to the standard of the original.

Chinese Army Uniforms, Equipment and Weaponry, 1931-1949

The U.S. supplied M-1917 Enfield .30-06 rifle which was commonly known as the P-17 was supplied in large numbers to the Chinese under the United States Lend Lease programme from 1941. It was the most common rifle in service with the U.S. trained Chinese divisions in India and was the standard model used by them in Burma in 1944-1945.

The German MP-18I along with later modifications was the first type of sub-machine gun in service with the Chinese from the 1920s. Later models like the Bergman MP-28 were manufactured in Germany and in Switzerland by SIG. China had already had a large number of the MP-18I in service with warlord armies and these were added to by the Nationalists after 1928.

Soldiers of the White Sun

The Mauser C-96 'Broomhandle' pistol was imported in huge quantities in the 1920s and 1930s into China. An Arms Embargo on the importation of rifles into China by the main powers was got around by selling the C-96 with a detachable wooden stock. This adaptation created a lightweight and practical pistol carbine which was ideally suited to the Chinese. Cheaper versions of the C-96 were produced by several Spanish manufacturers and were also exported to China in large numbers.

Opposite top: U.S. made Thompson sub-machine guns were a popular if expensive addition to the Chinese armoury. The original M-1921 model was imported in small numbers by the Nationalist government in the early-1930s. However the vast majority of Thompson's seen in Chinese service before 1942 were copies made in several local arsenals. This example for instance was made in the Shensi Arsenal and has a much longer muzzle than the original. Most Chinese produced copies were noticeably cruder in manufacture but were still used by the Nationalists even when new Lend Lease supplied Thompson's were sent by the U.S.

Opposite bottom: ZB vz26 7.92mm light machine guns were manufactured by the Brno Company in Czechoslovakia and became the standard weapon of this type in Chinese service. The ZB vz26 was imported in large numbers from 1927 to 1939 with the figure of 30,249 quoted by Brno. These were later supplemented by the slightly improved ZB vz30 and a large number of copies which were made in several Chinese government arsenals.

This Type-24 7.92mm heavy machine gun is a Chinese made version of the German DWM Maxim M1909 which was commercial version the M1908. The German military mission in China during the early to mid-1930s arranged for the setting up of a factory to produce the Type-24. Altogether there were over 36,000 of this type of machine gun produced in China and it continued in service until 1949 with the Nationalists and then into the 1960s with the Communists. In the photograph we can see both the water can to feed the water-cooling system around the barrel and a box of ammunition.